Drawn & Colored
by
Lilan Chen

"Global Doodle Gems"
Mini Collection Volume 5

Share your colored versions with us !

The Official FB book page, stay on top of what we have in the works !
www.facebook.com/globaldoodlegems

The Community group, share your colored pages, meet the artists, enjoy exclusive freebies, take part in community Charity books and so much more......
www.facebook.com/groups/globaldoodlegems/

Follow us on Twitter.... @GlobalDoodlegem

We are on Instagram too
@globaldoodlegems for instagram

...and if you are not social like that we have a blog
globaldoodlegems.wordpress.com

Copyright © 2015 Global Doodle Gems
Published by Global Doodle Gems
      Anna-Marie Vibeke Wedel

All rights are reserved by Global Doodle Gems.

Duplication of pages for personal use are allowed. You are invited to color the pages then scan/post your coloured versions to social networks, mentioning the book title and author/artist
(Global Doodle Gems).

All artwork and images are protected by copyright laws. This book or any portion thereof may not, otherwise, be reproduced and/or distributed or transmitted without the express written permission of the artist/publisher of Global Doodle Gems.

All of us from the Global Doodle Gems wish you a colortastic time and look forward to seeing your wonderful color results online !

Published by "GDG" Global Doodle Gems

Contributing Artists
"Global Doodle Gems"
Mini Collection Volume 5

Thank you for your contributions

Leen Margot, Johanna Ans,
Alfred E. Villanueva, Arianne Schimmel,
Audrey Sagh, Bev Choy,
Diana Holmes, Joann Sands,
Jodi Ho, Lilan Chen,
Lynne McGee, Nancy 43,
Pica Wu, Rover Hsiao, T.J.,
Mireille W.
and
Nadège Zenfeerie

Contributing Artist
Leen Margot
France

Facebook Group : https://www.facebook.com/groups/666909036736080/

More Books : http://www.alittlemarket.com/dessins/fr_offre_speciale_saint_valentin_une_boite_de_feutres_maped_colorpep_s_brush_offerte_avec_ma_pause_a_moi_et_mille_-12935453.html

Twitter : leenmargot

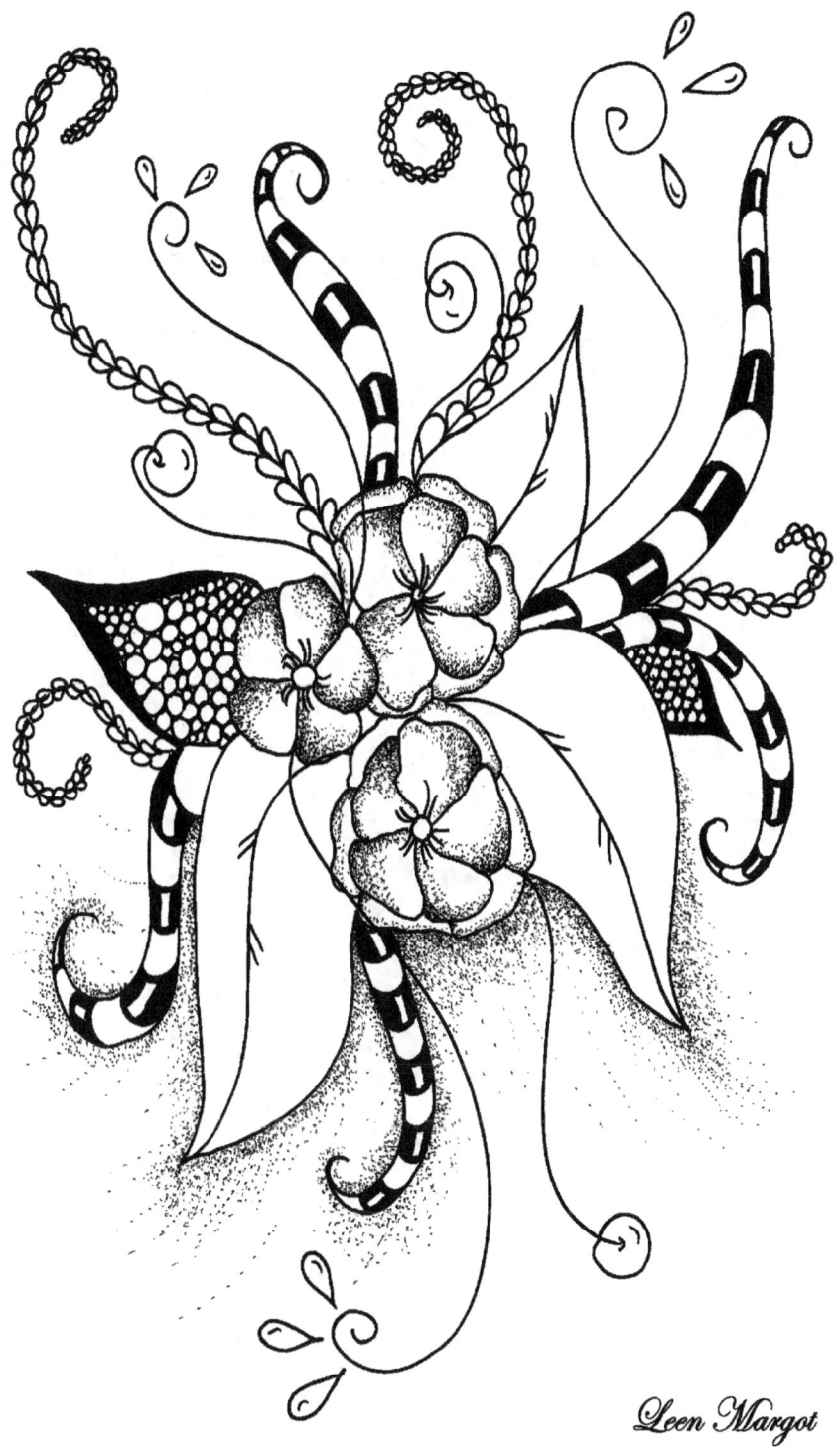

Contributing Artist
MWMS-Johanna Ans
The Netherlands

Blog : mywaymystylejohannaans.wordpress.com

Facebook : Johanna-Ans-My-creative-site

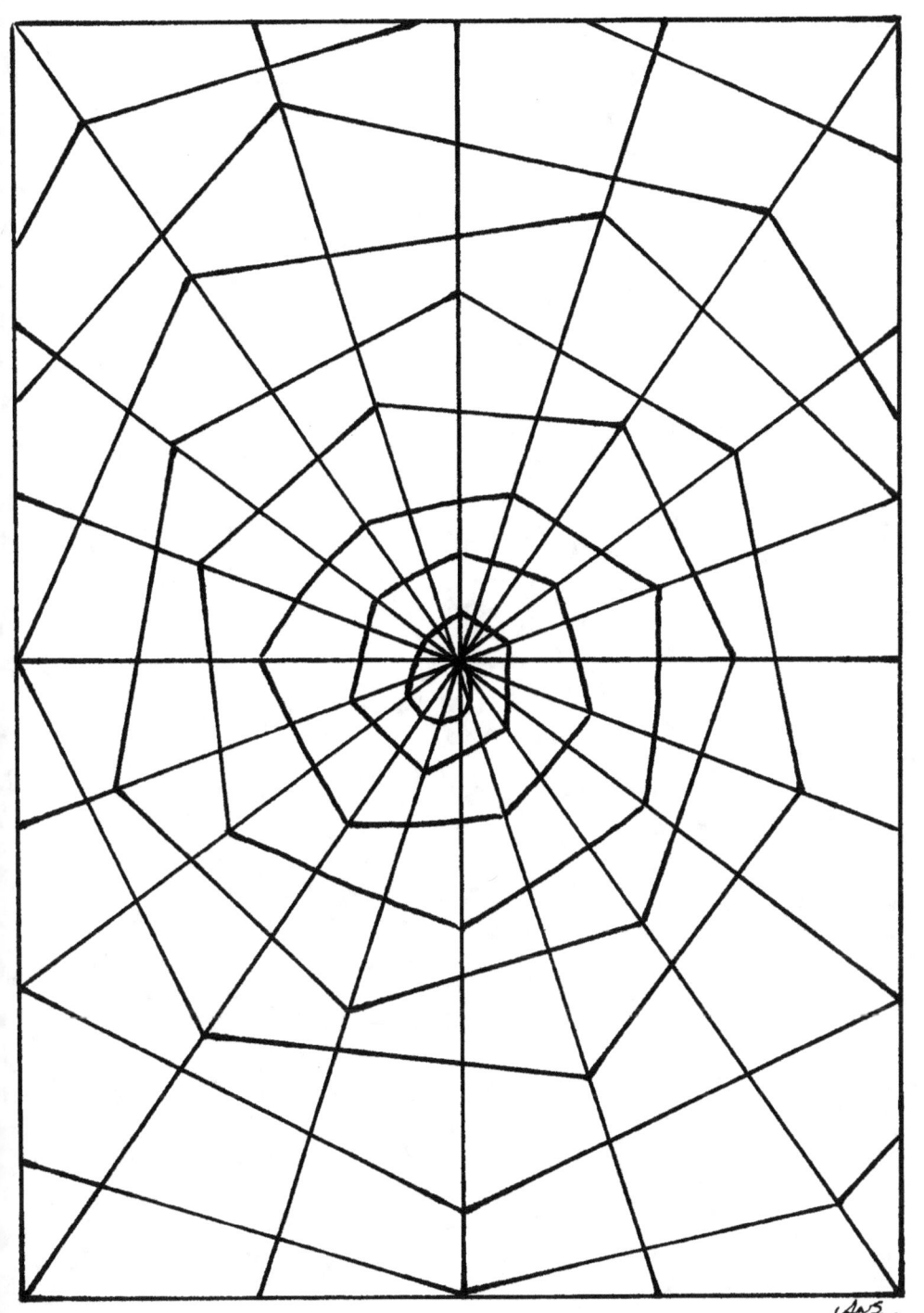

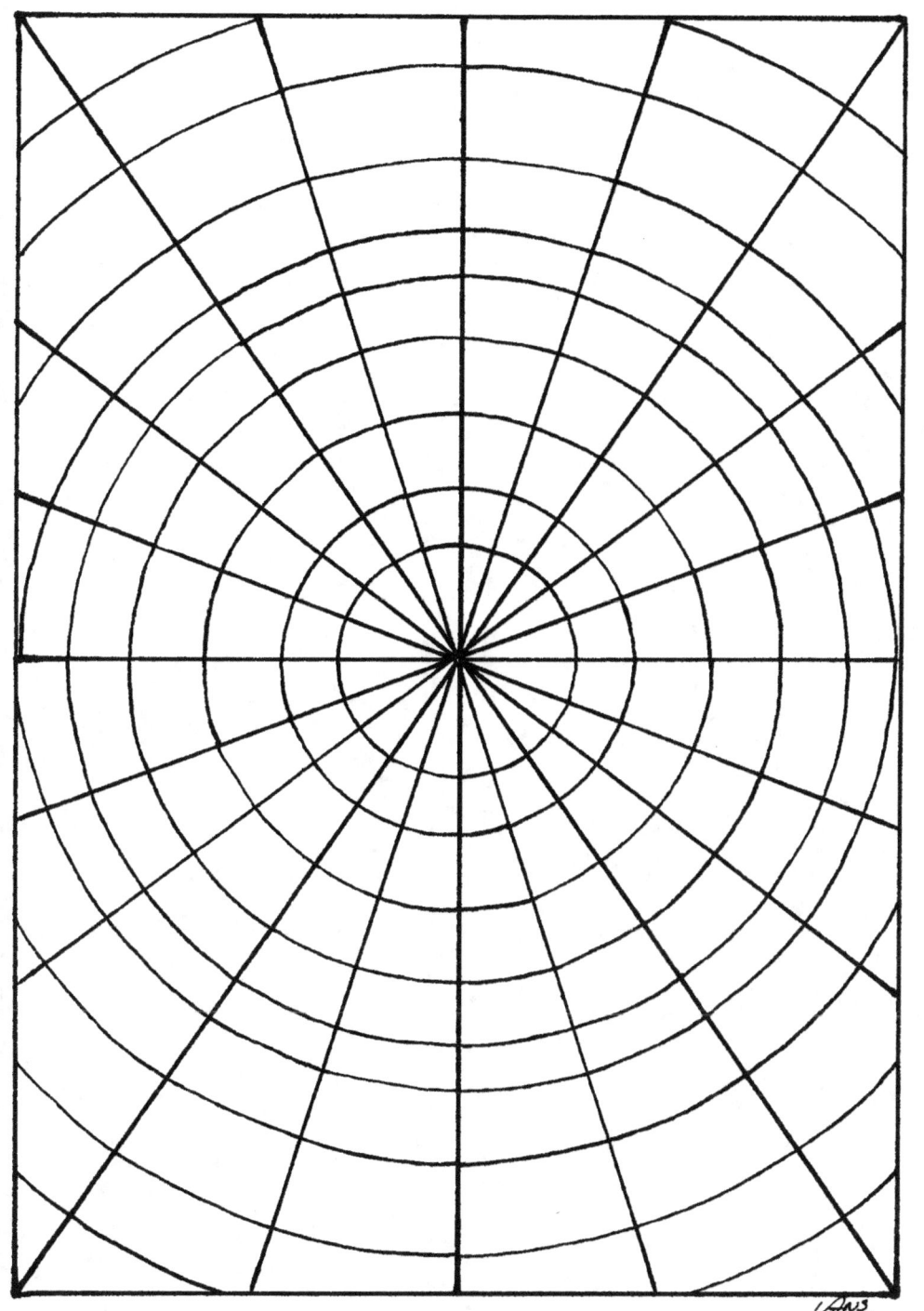

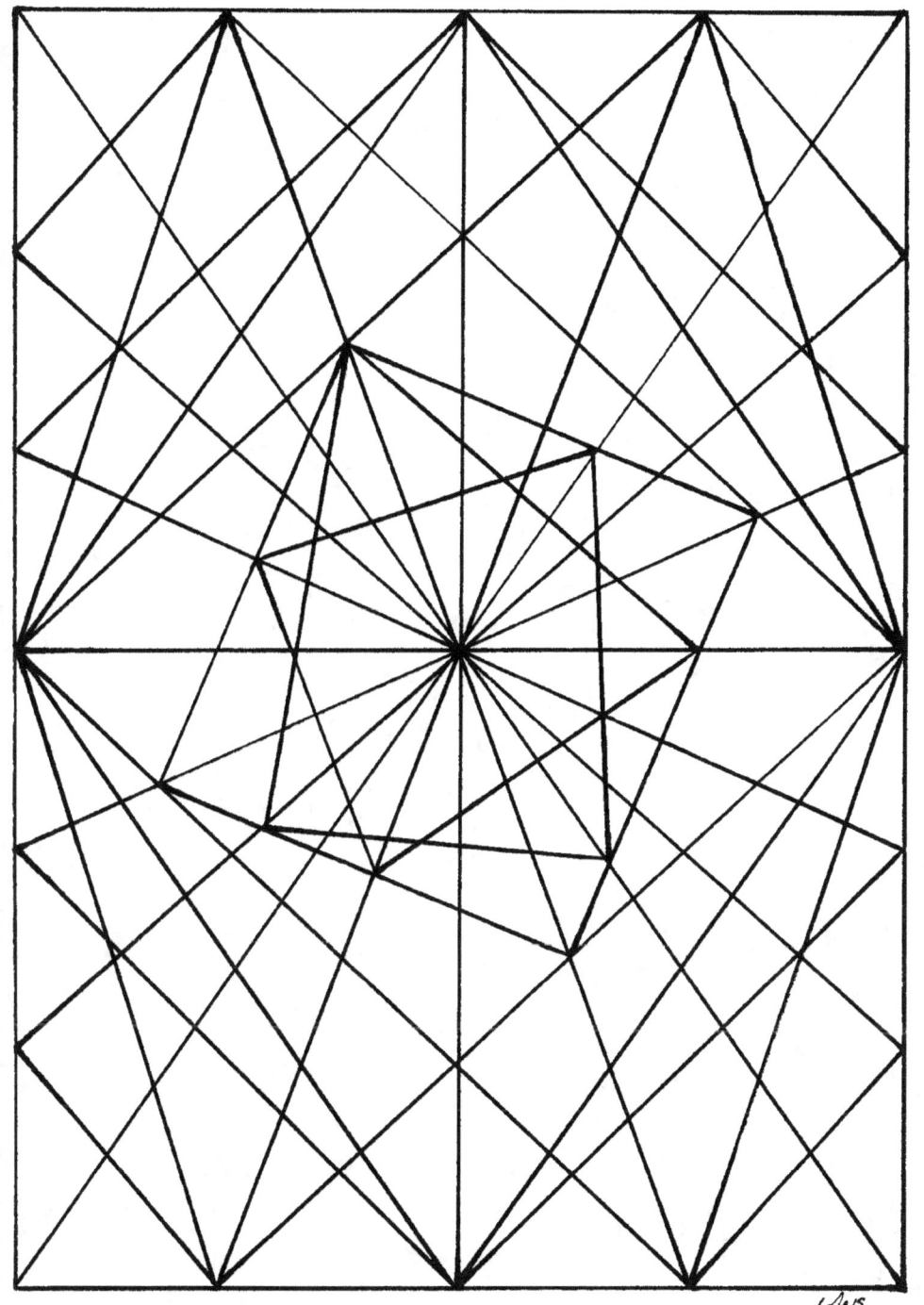

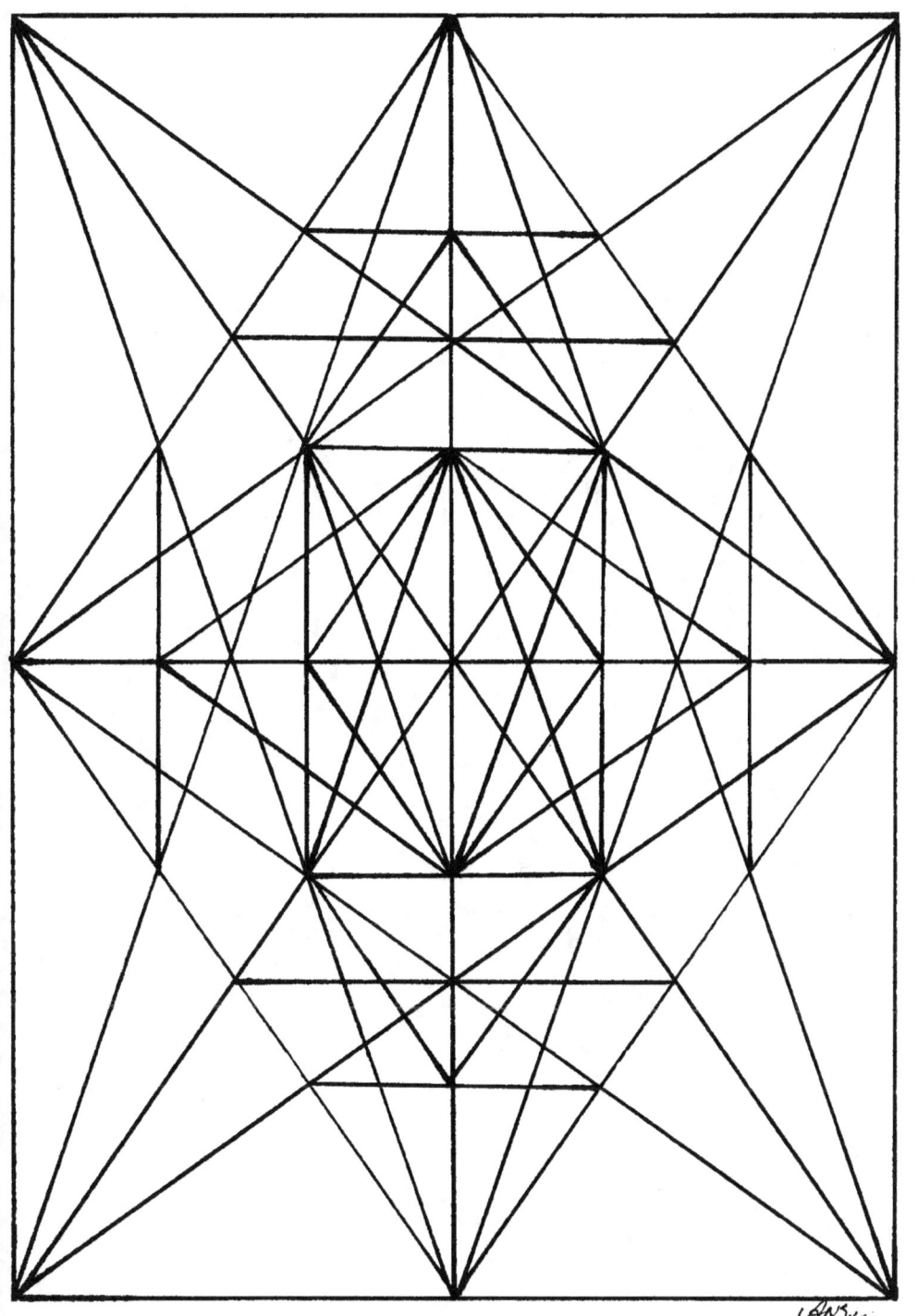

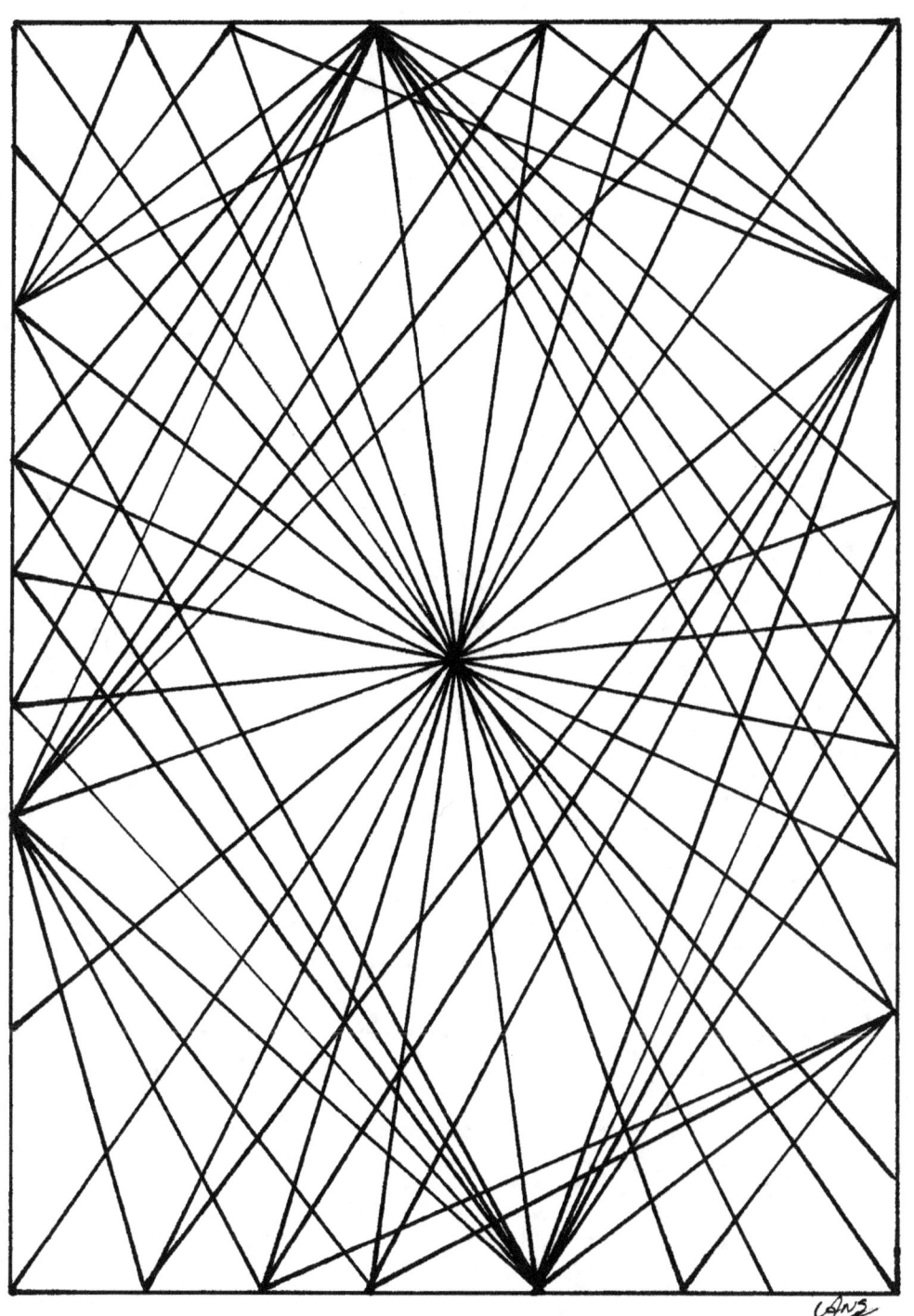

Contributing Artist
Alfred E. Villanueva
Philippines

Facebook : viworksart2015

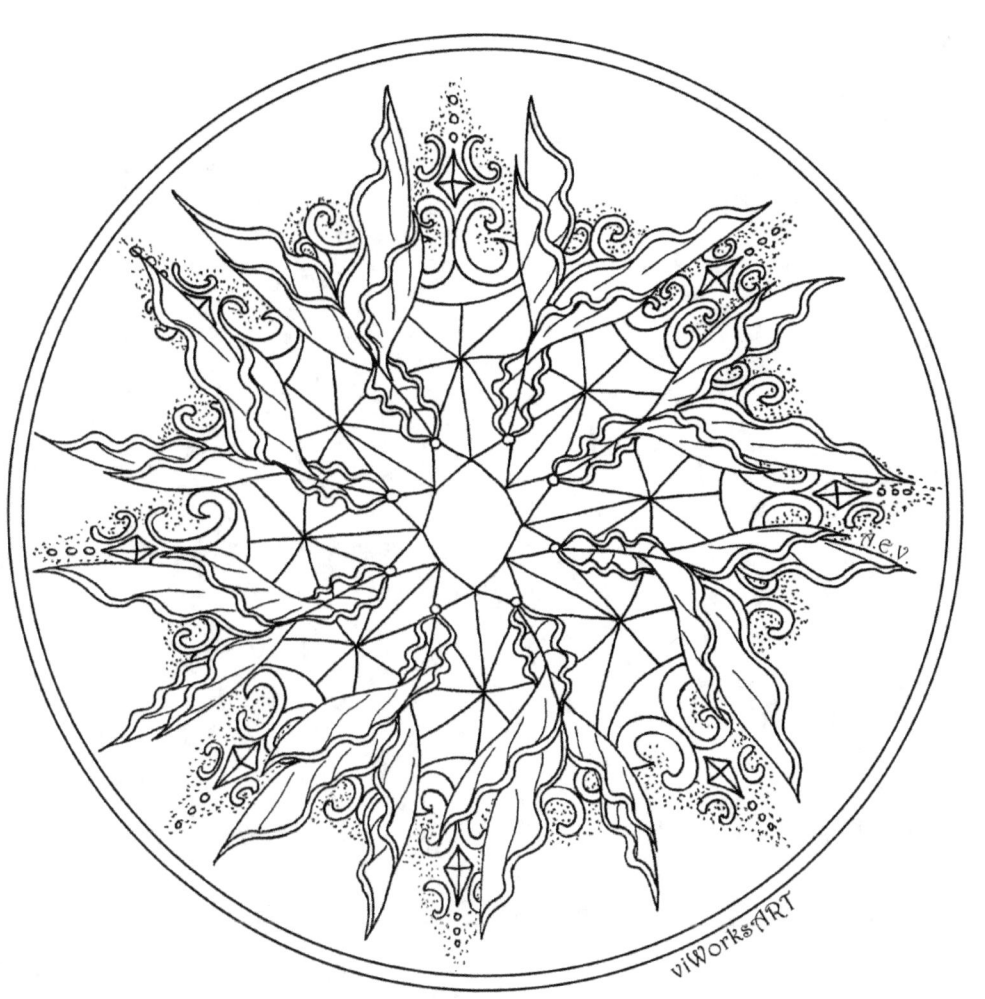

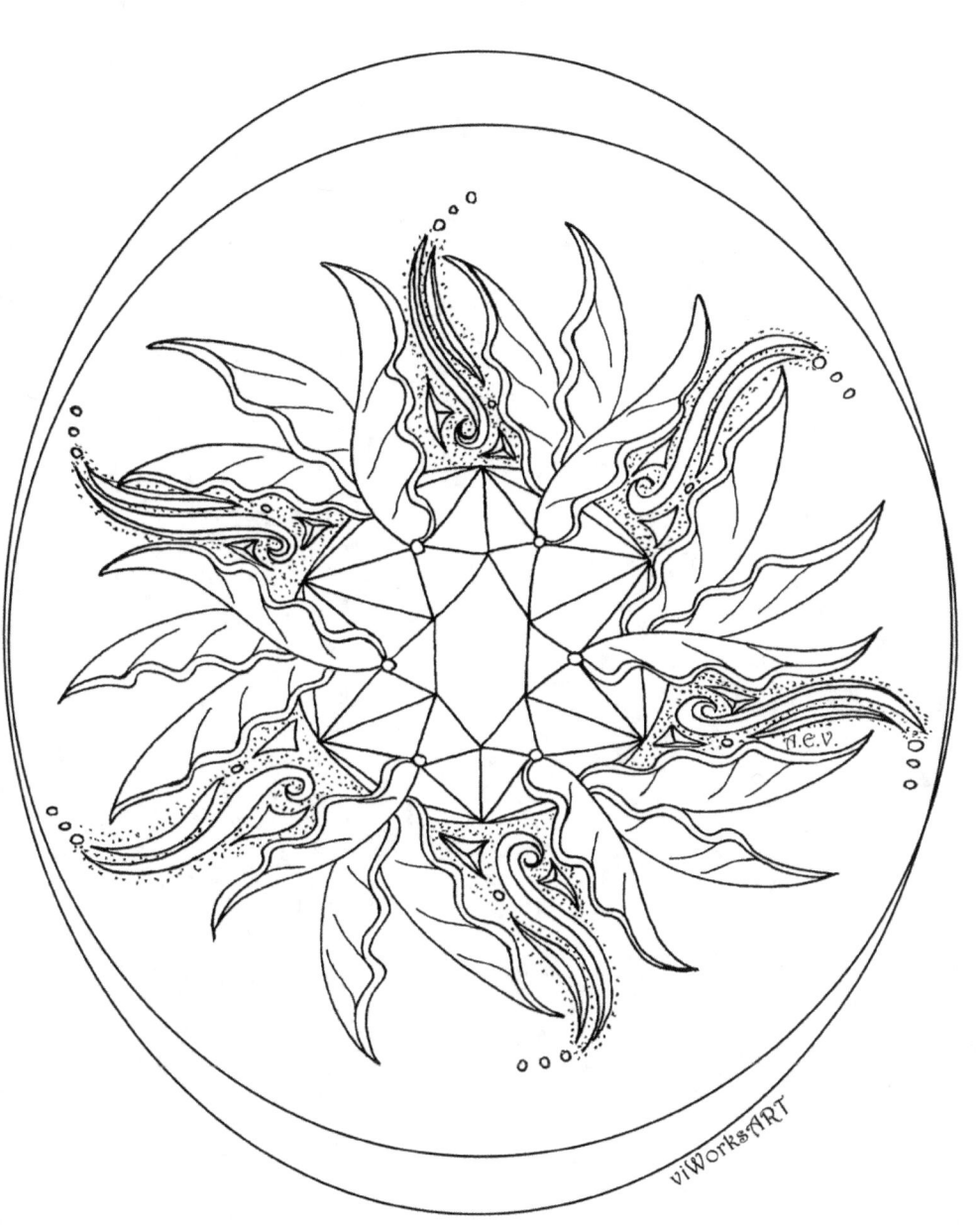

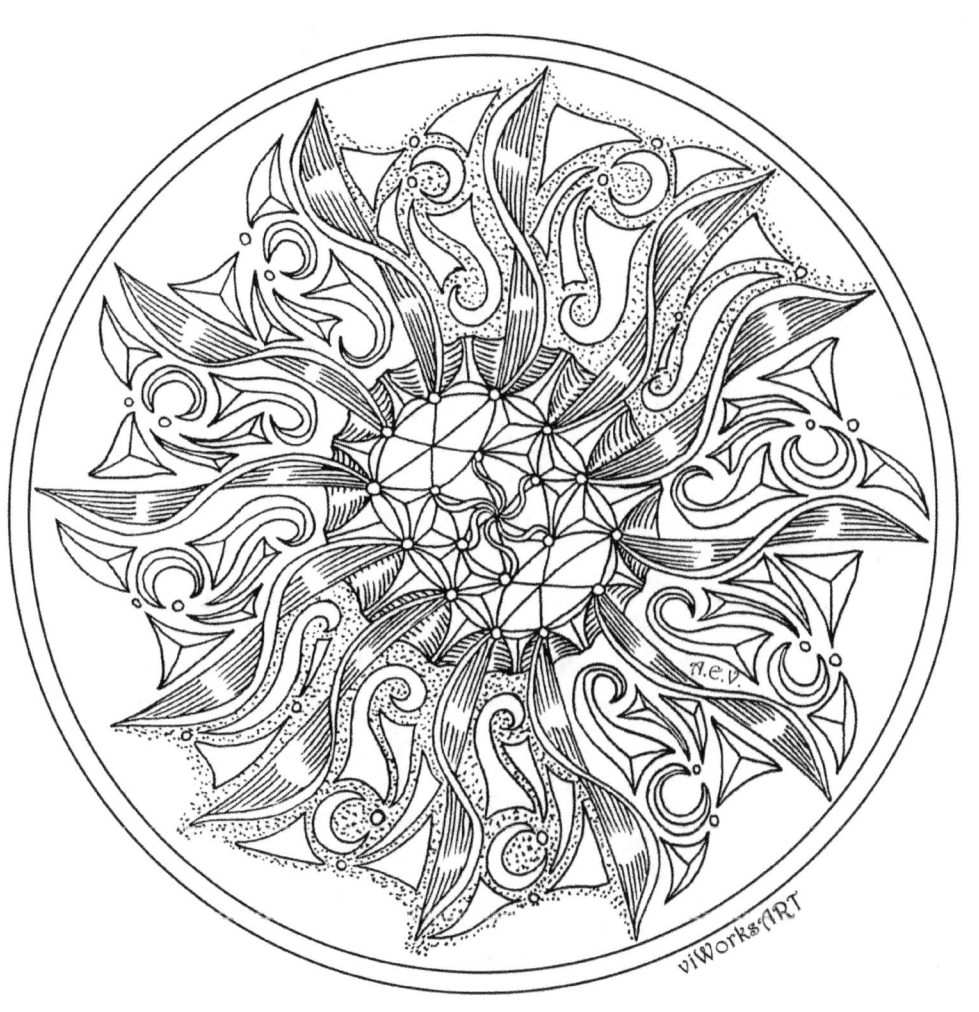

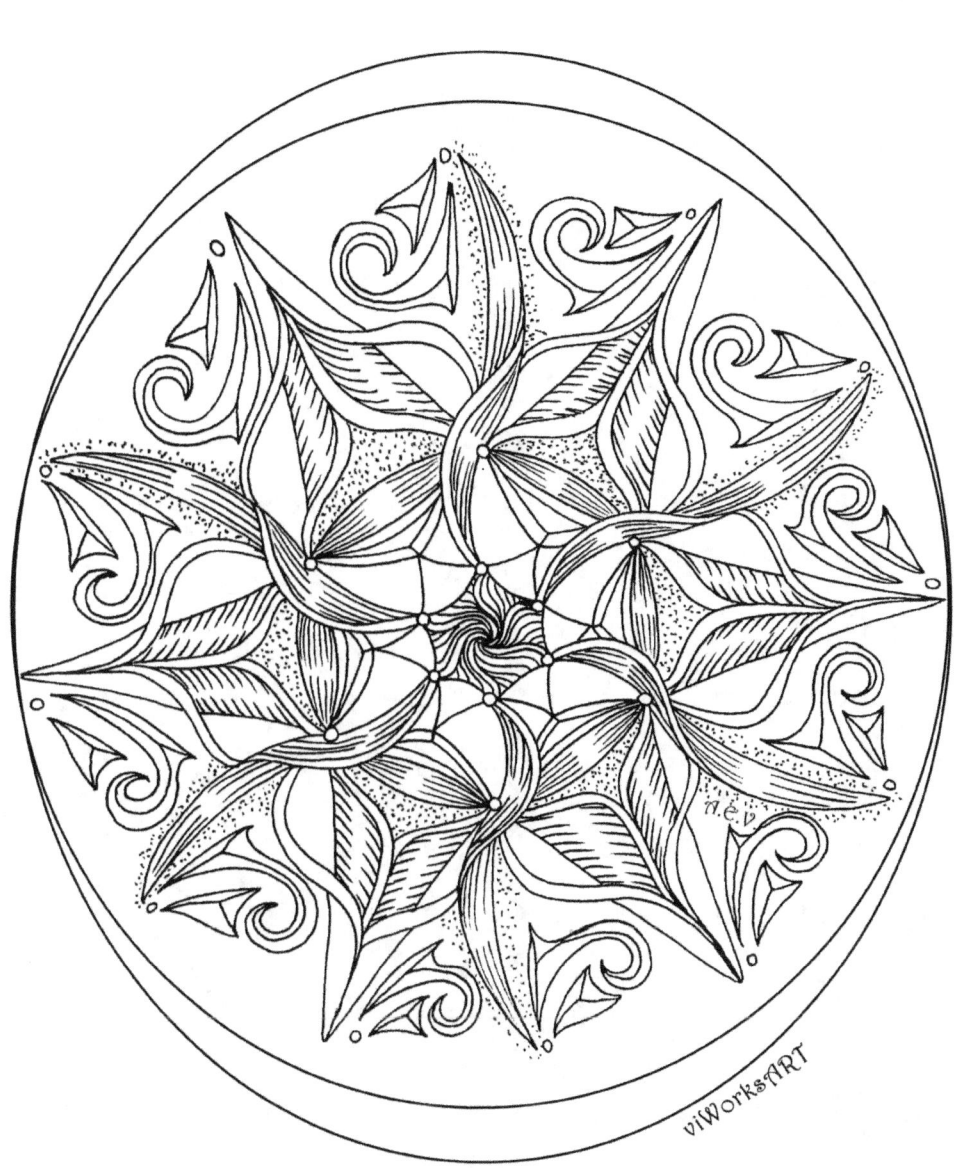

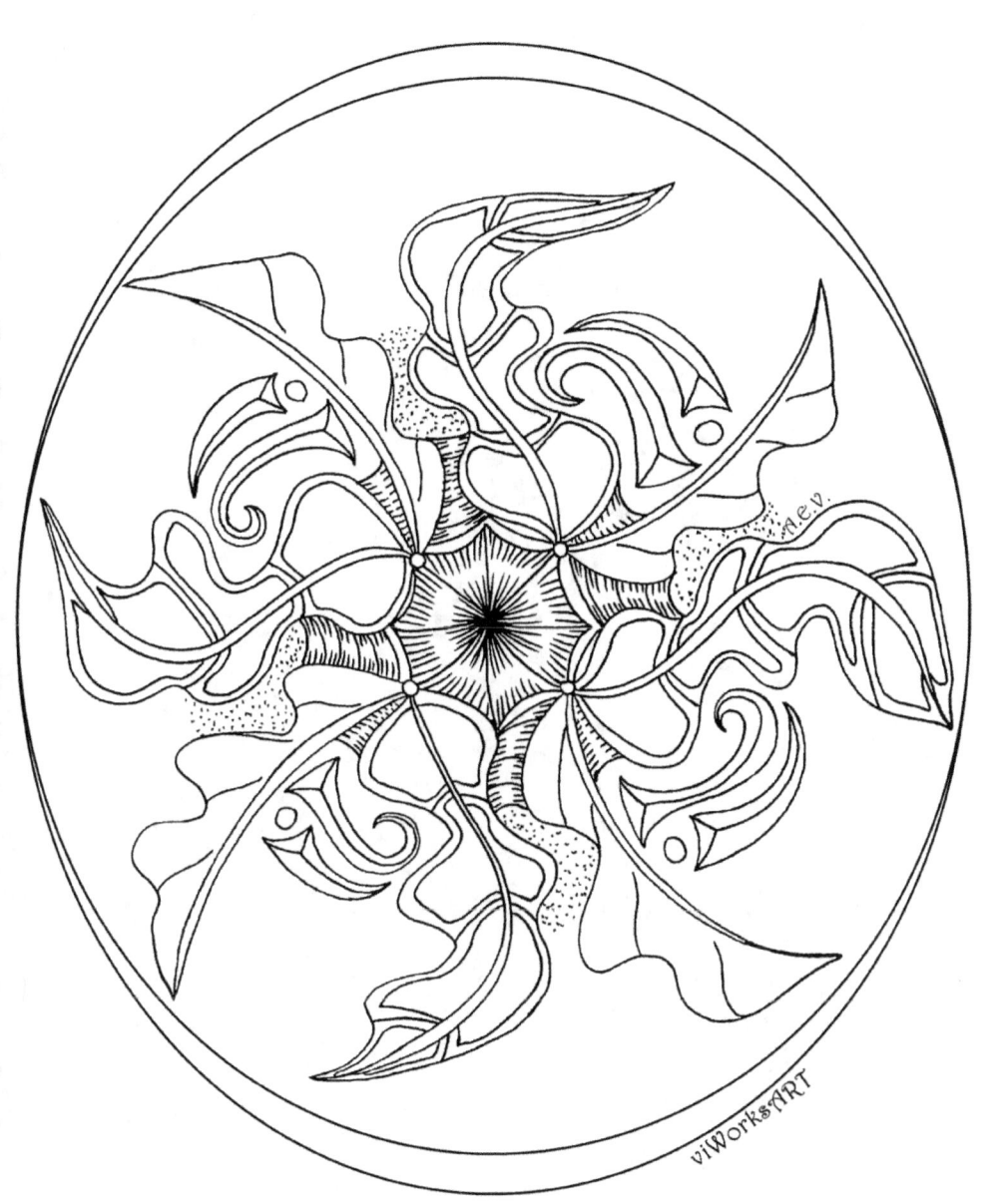

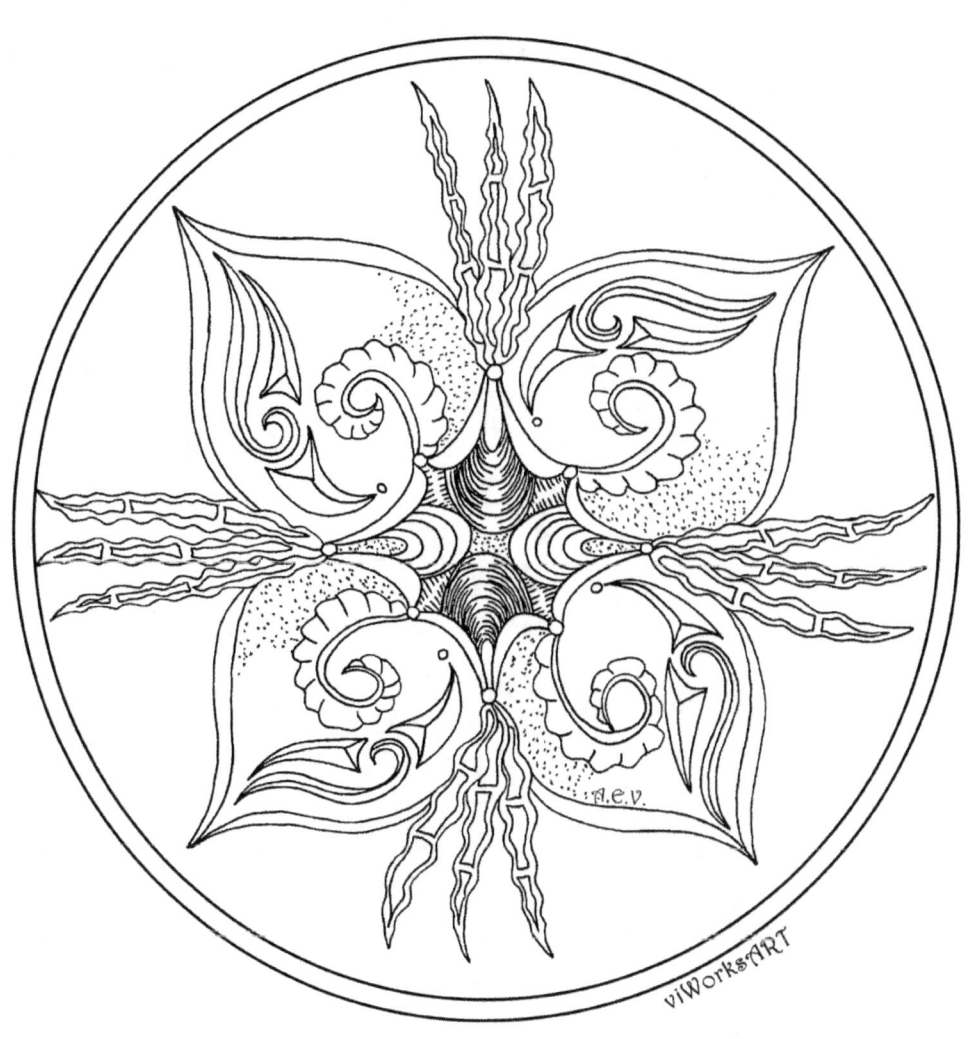

Contributing Artist
Arianne Schimmel
The Netherlands

Facebook : ArianneSchimmel

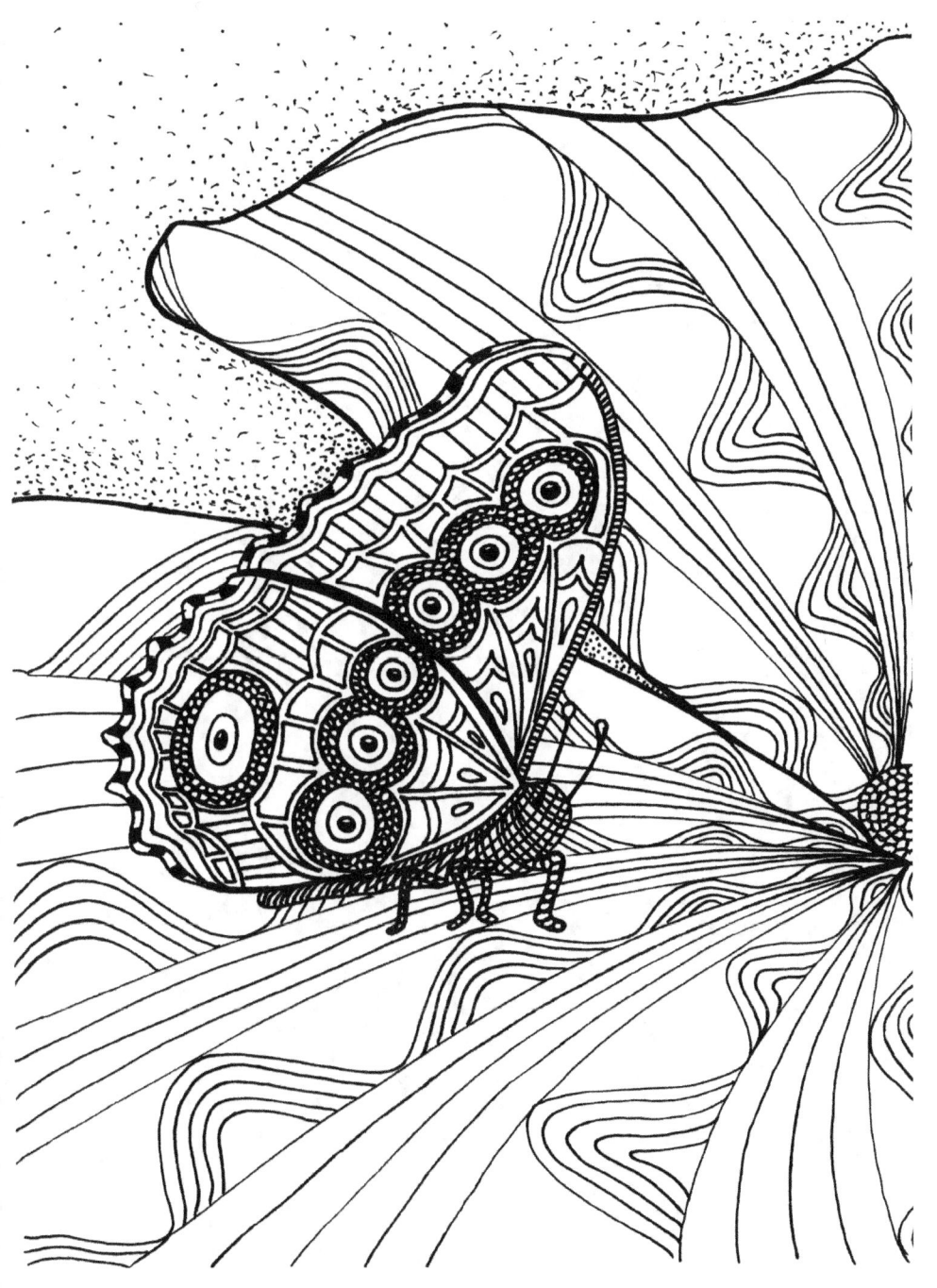

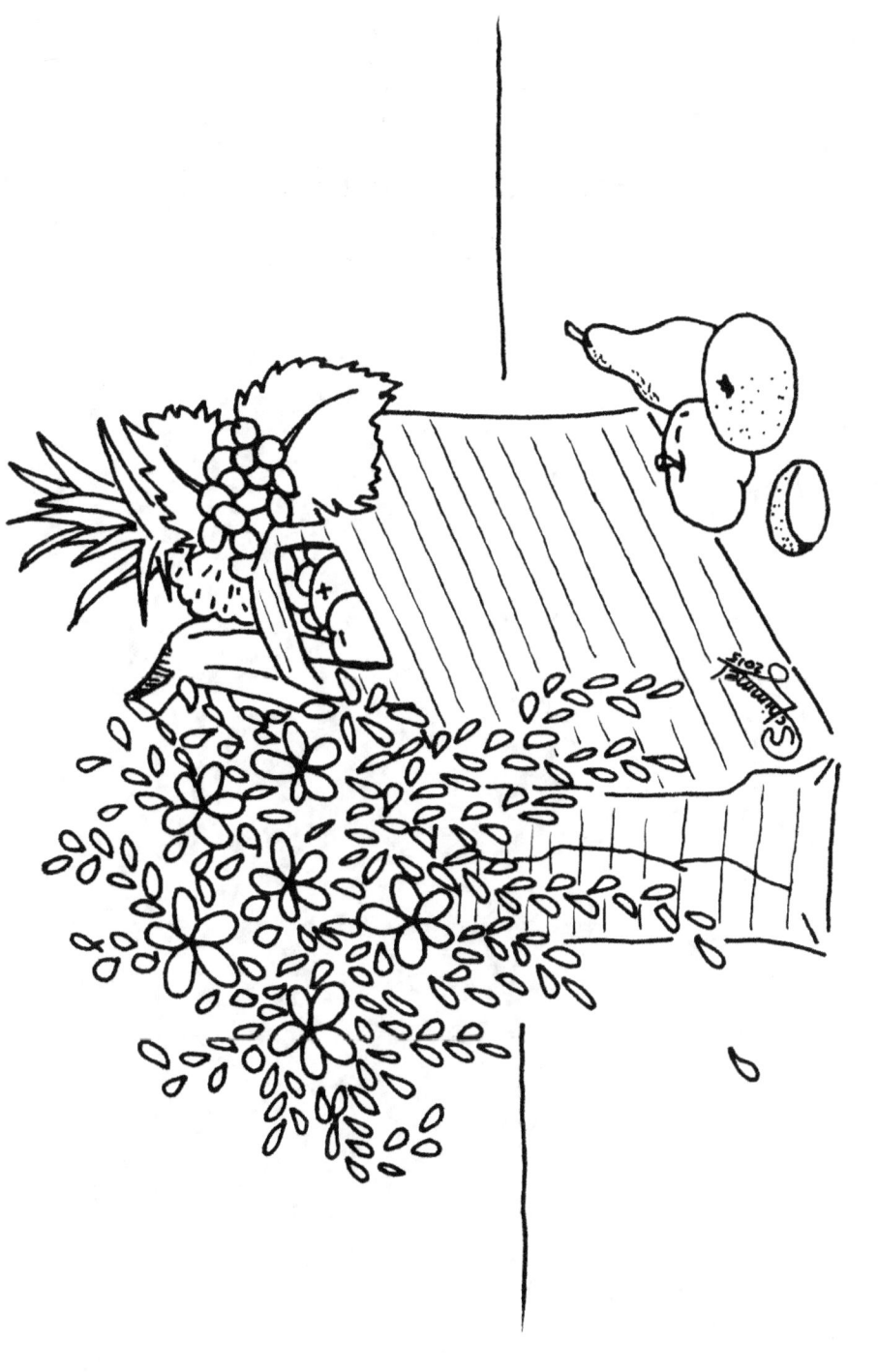

Contributing Artist
Audrey Sagh
Saskatoon, Saskatchewan Canada

Facebook : AMS-Artwork

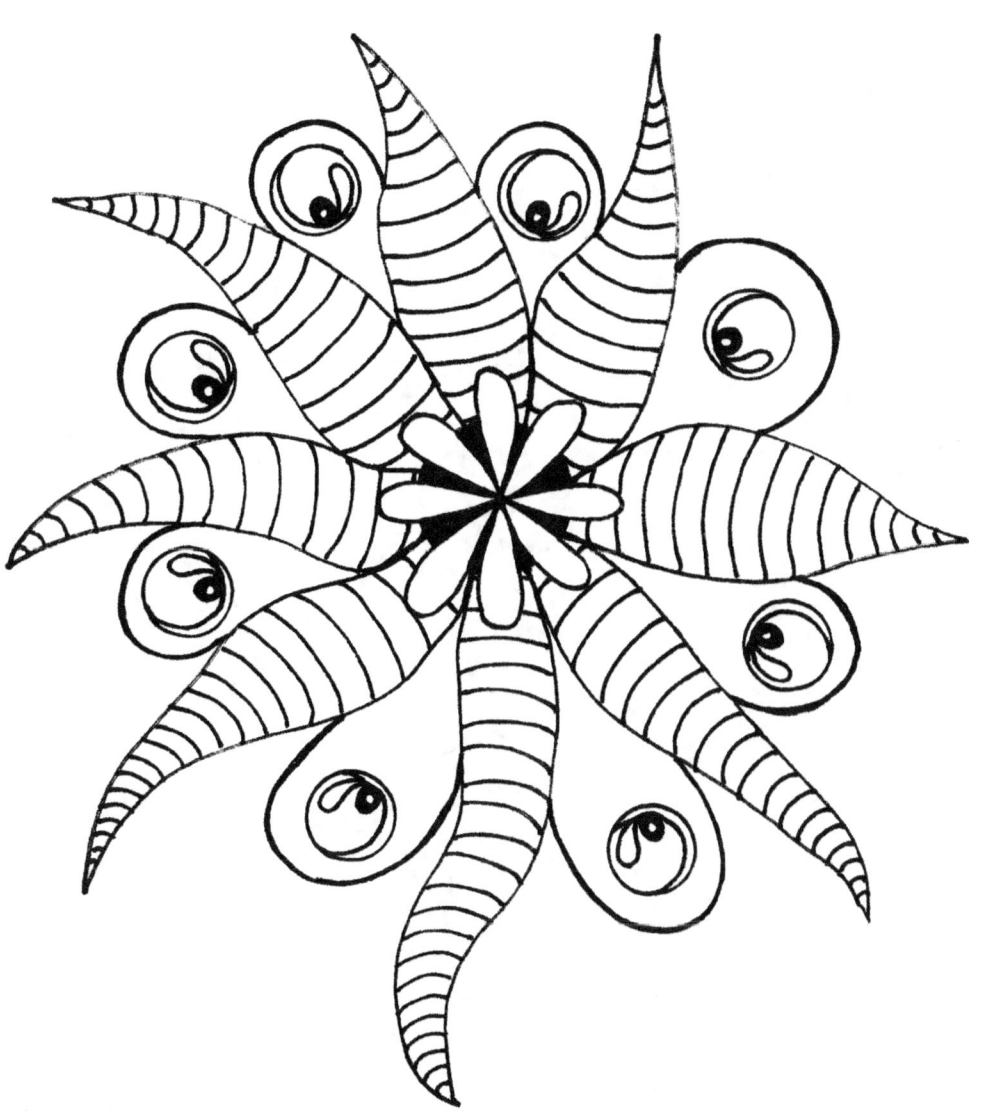

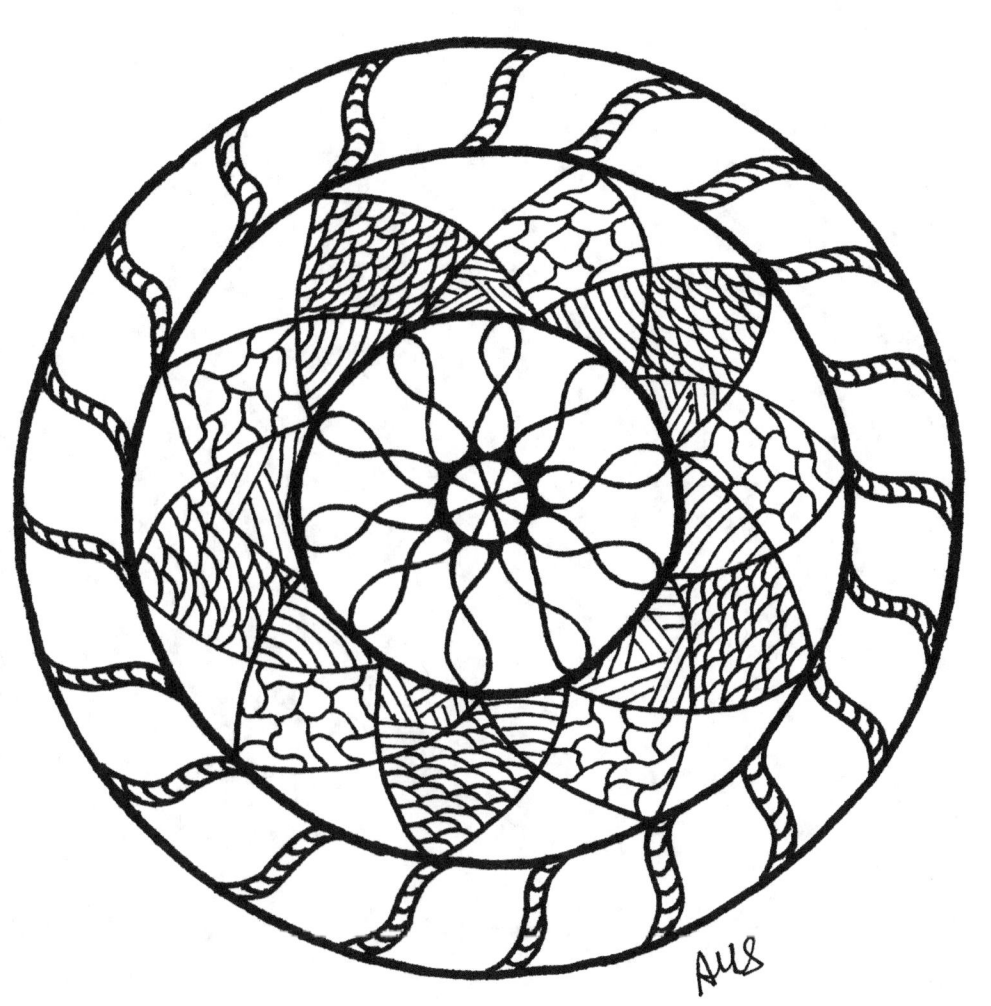

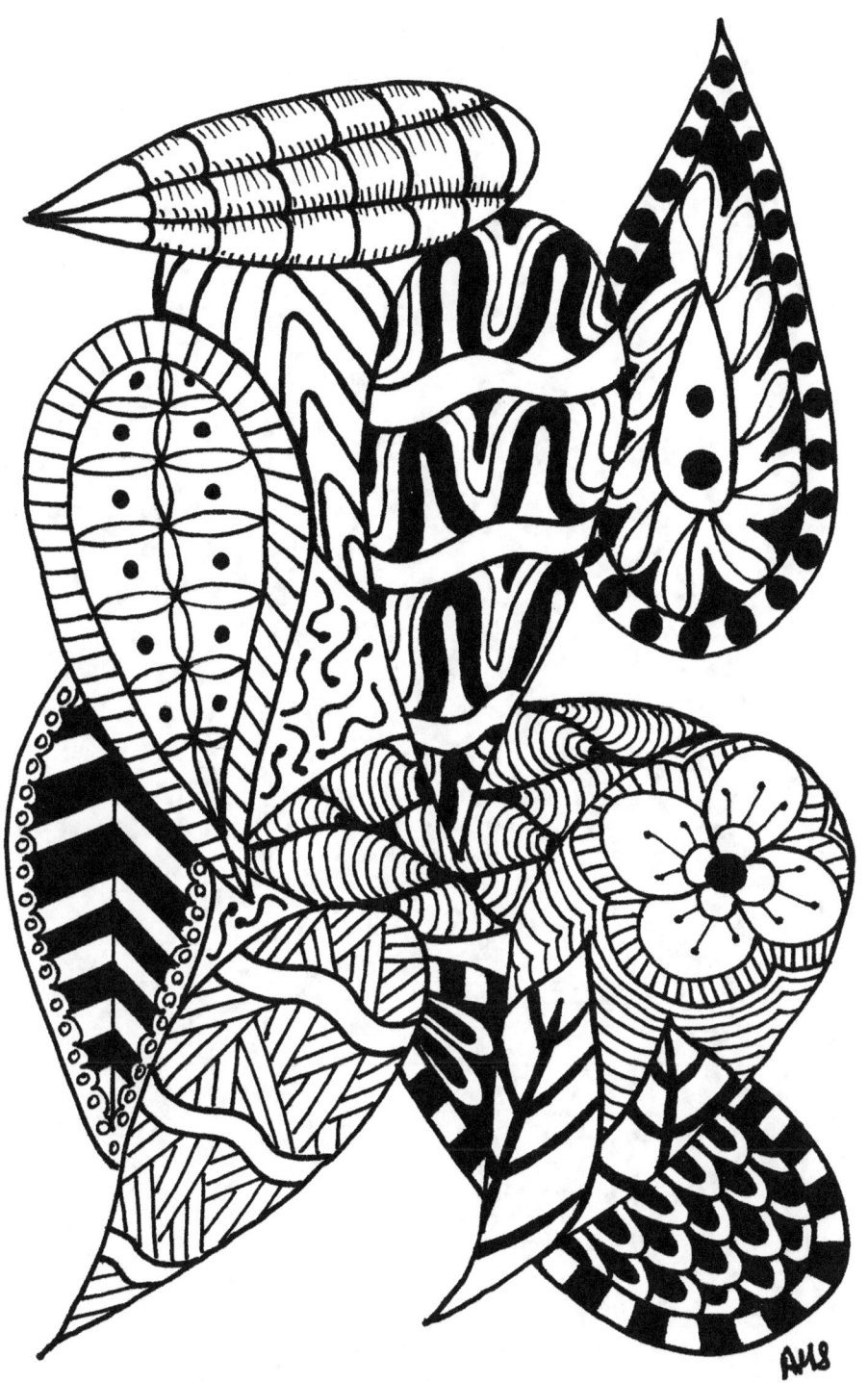

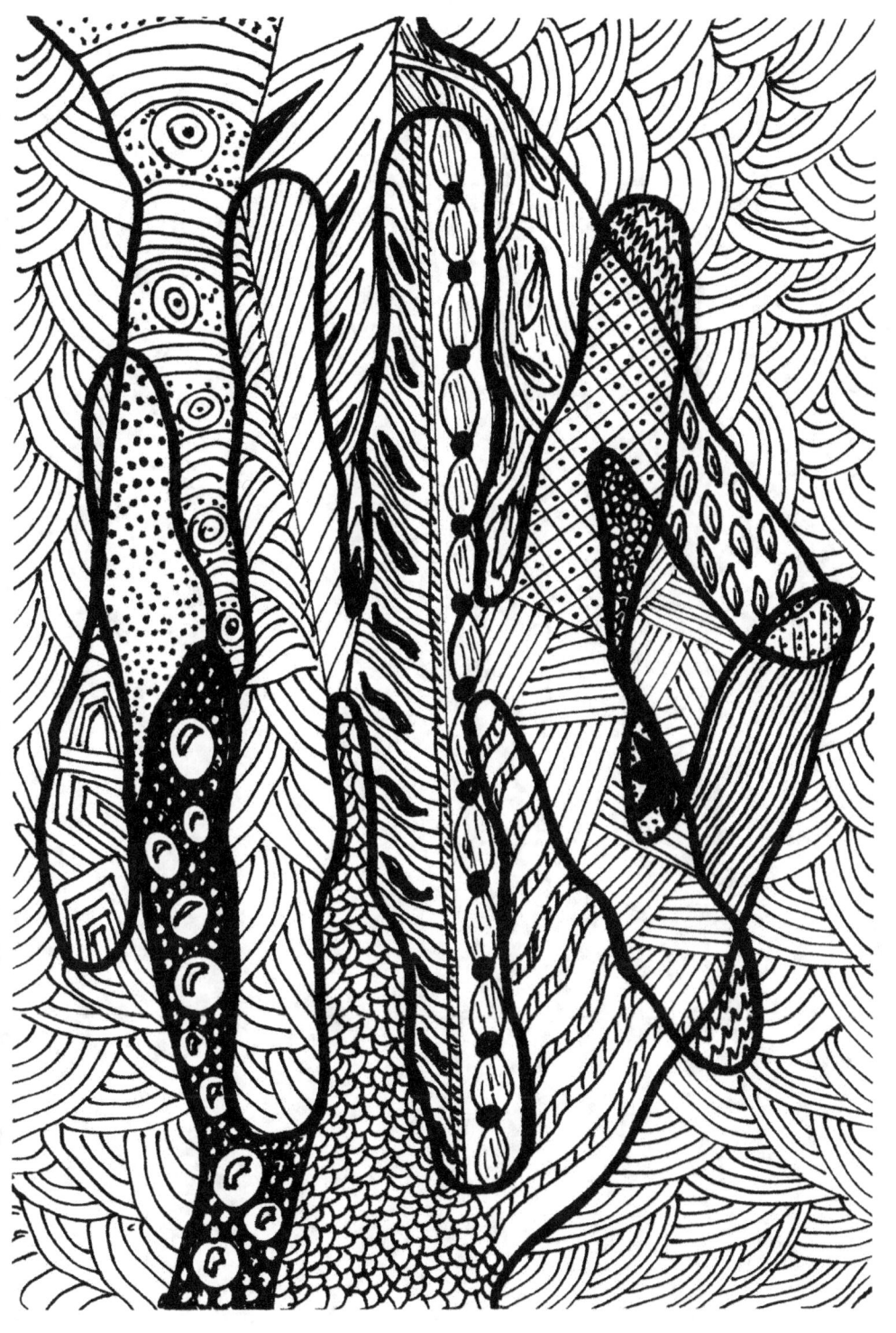

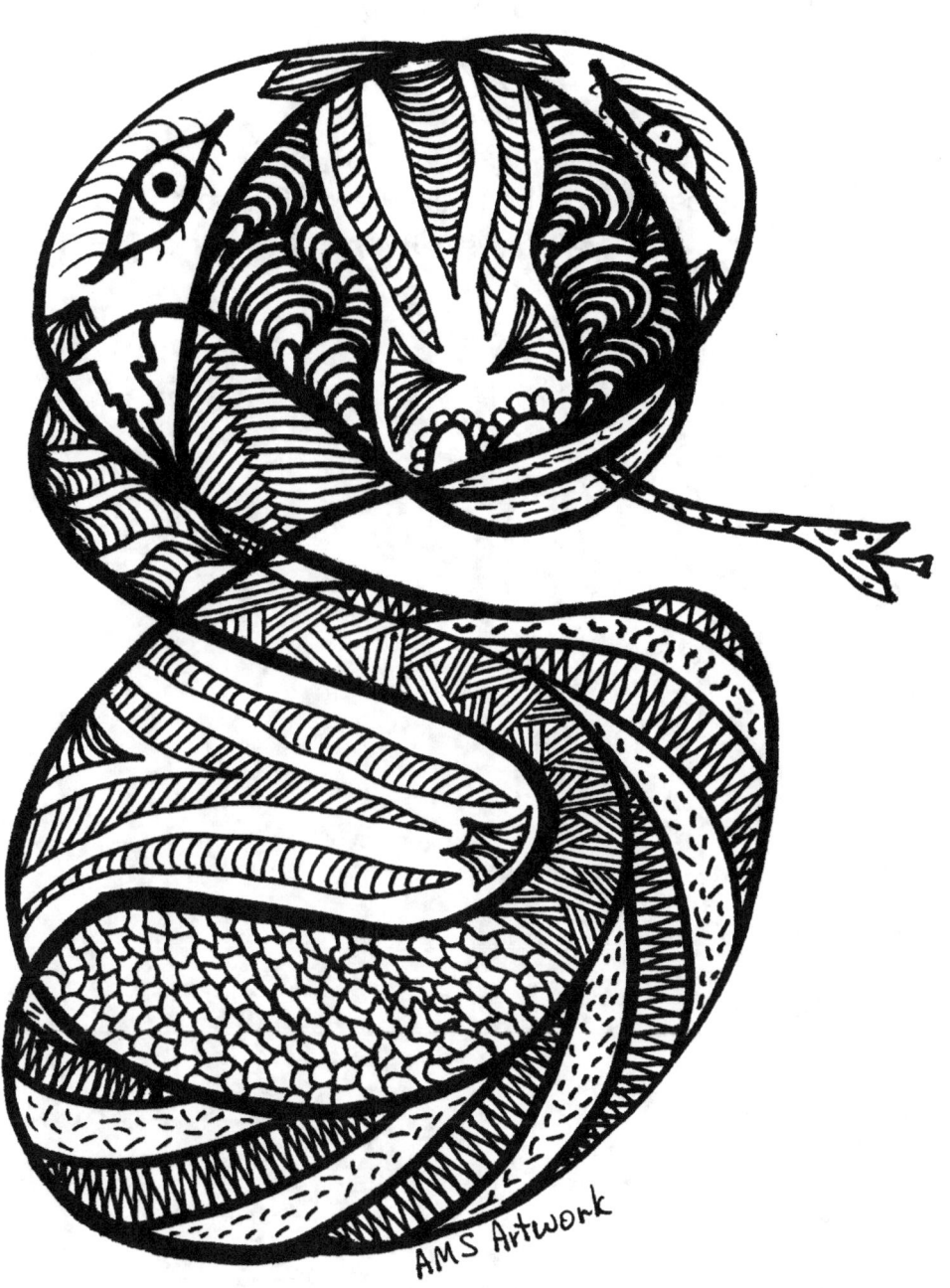

Contributing Artist
Bev Choy
USA

Facebook : bevchoyart
Facebook Group : MixedMediaSupport
Etsy : BevChoyArt

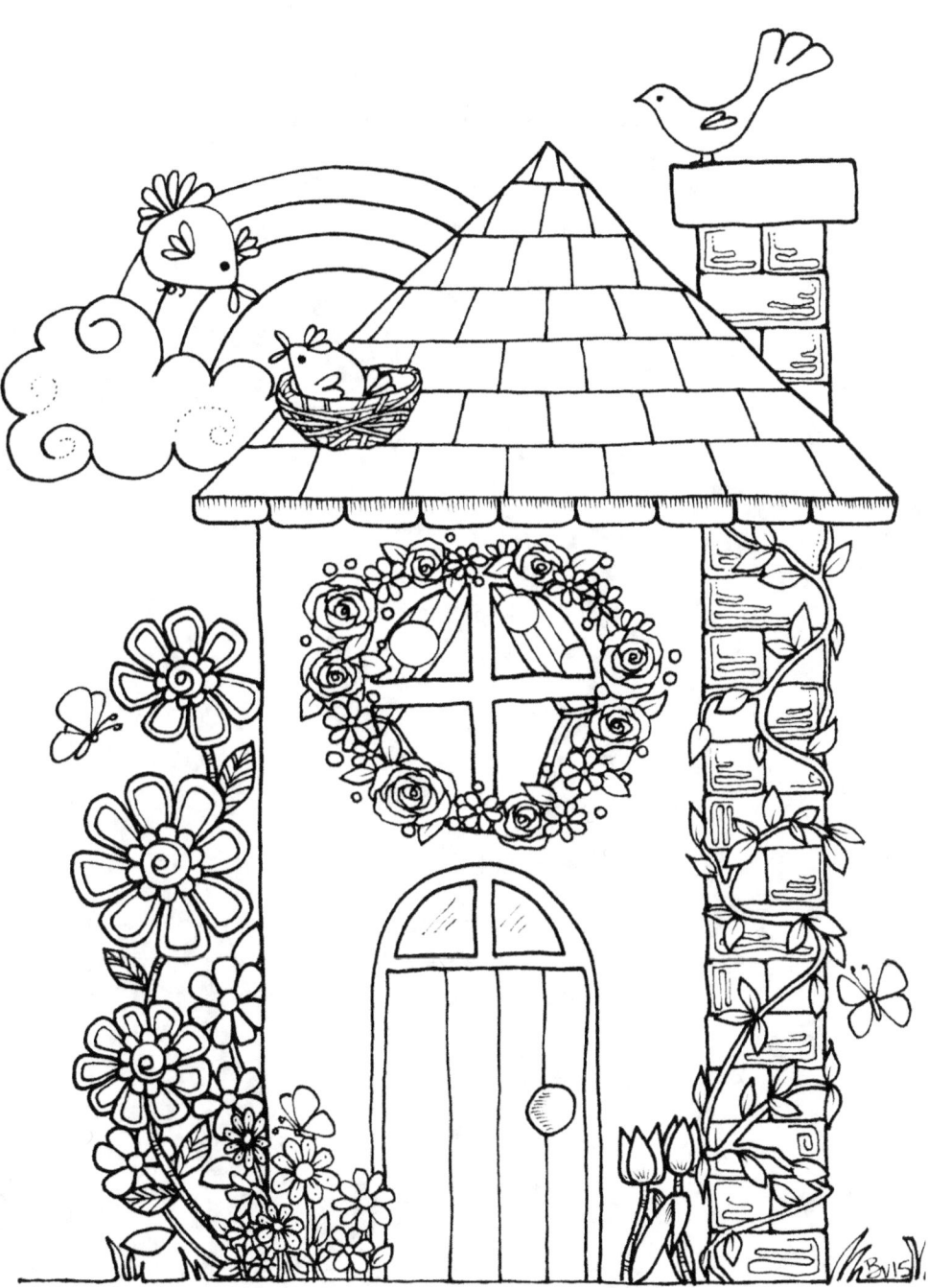

Contributing Artist
Diana Holmes
USA

Facebook : WhimsicalCheers

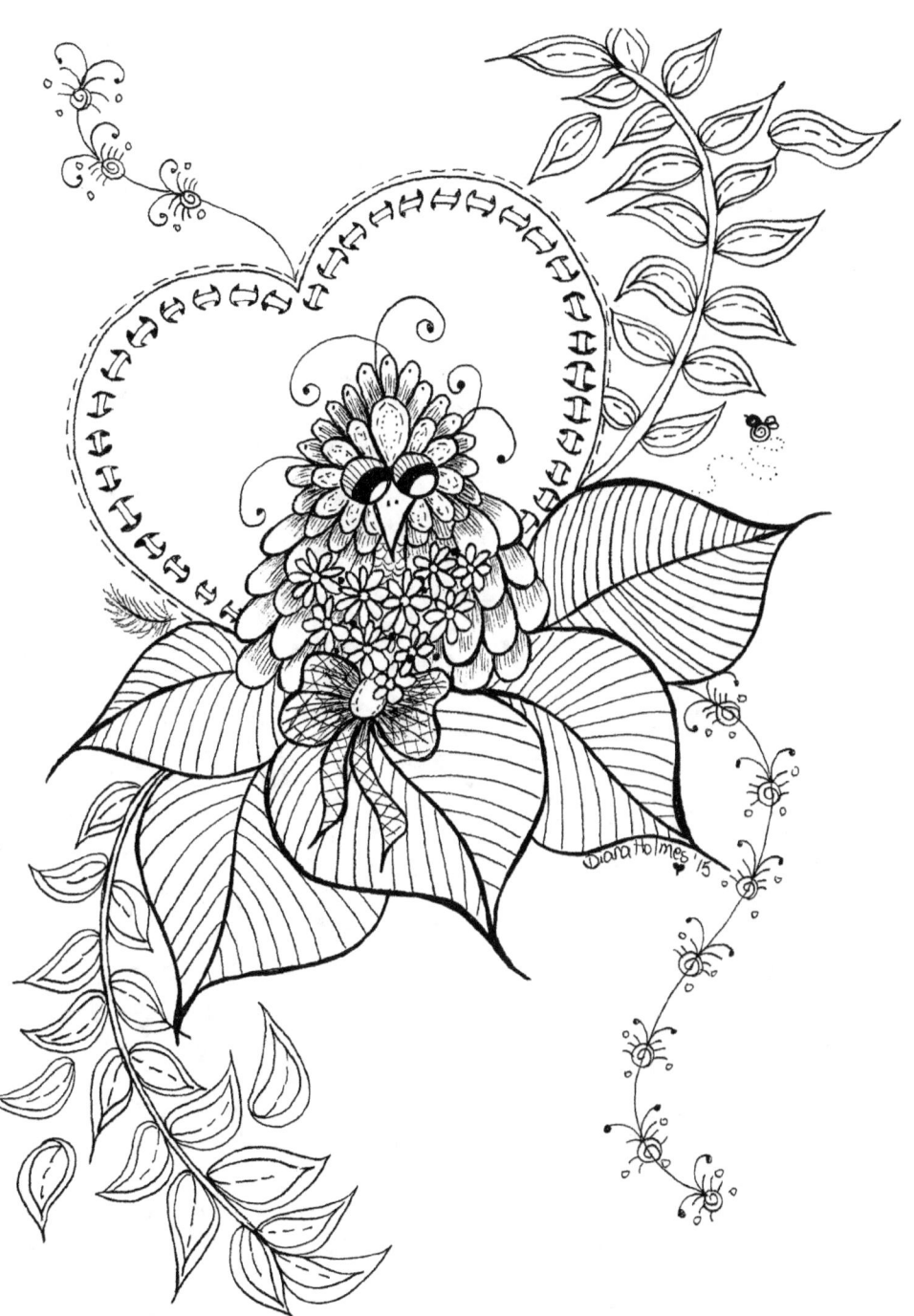

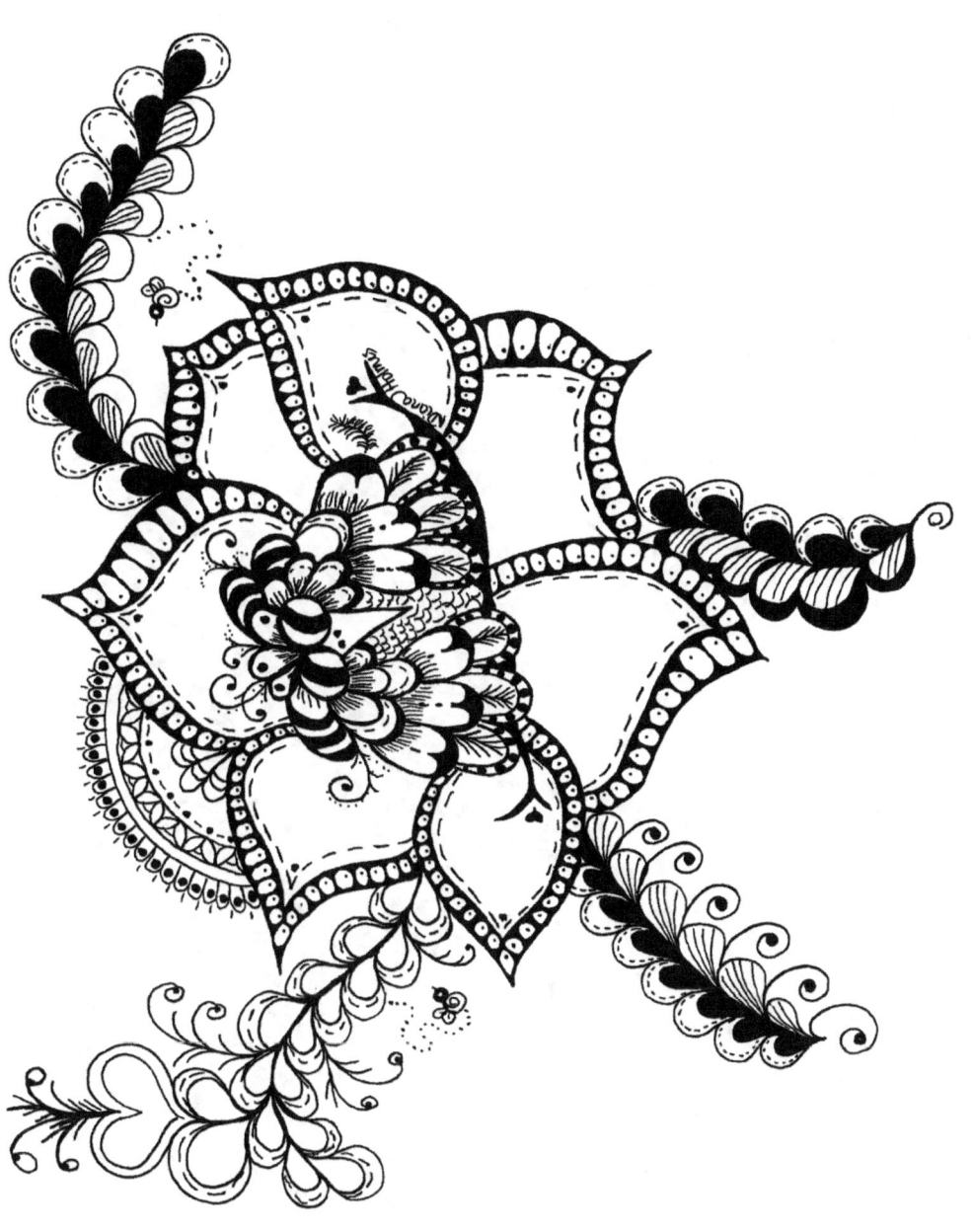

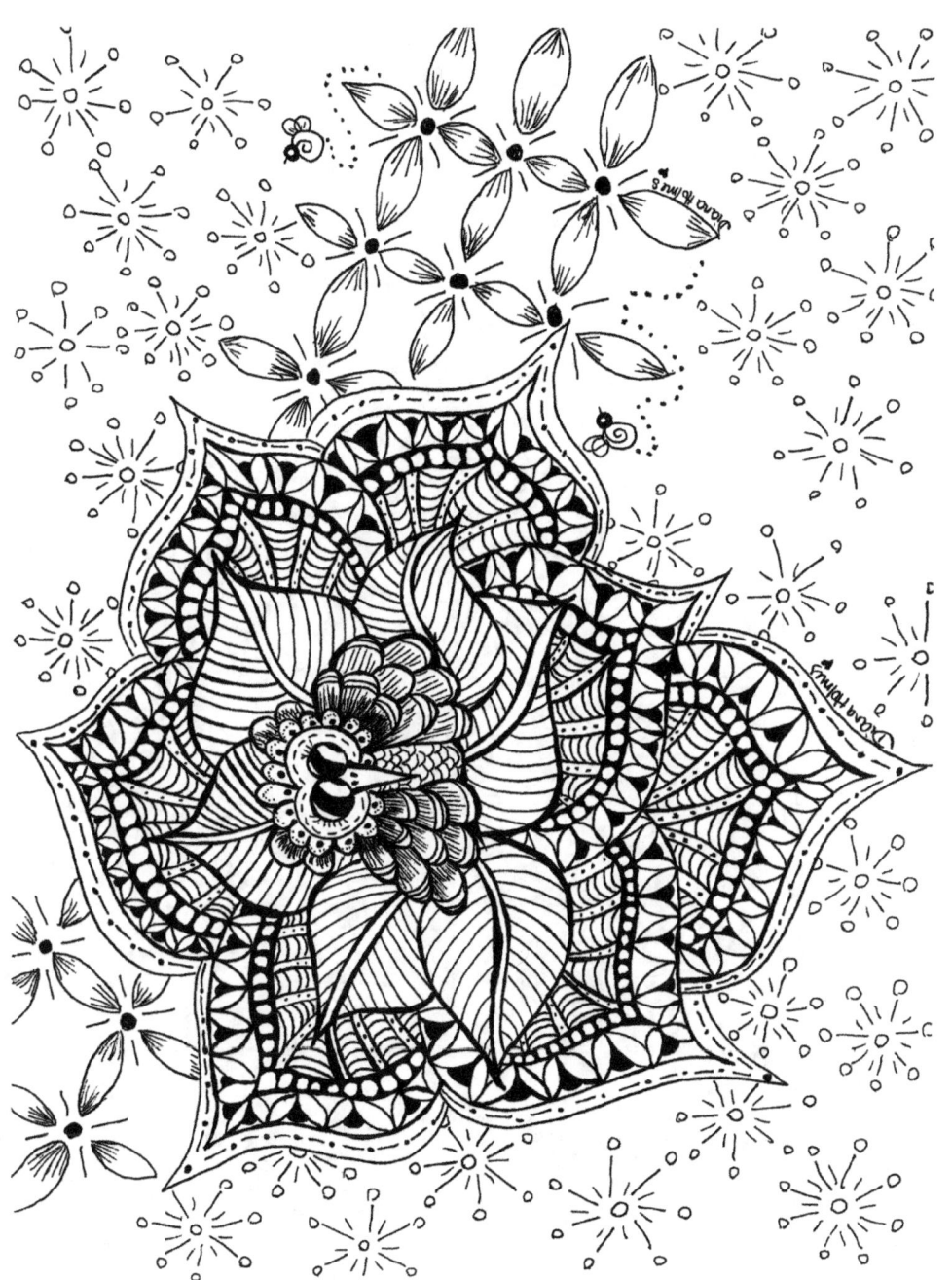

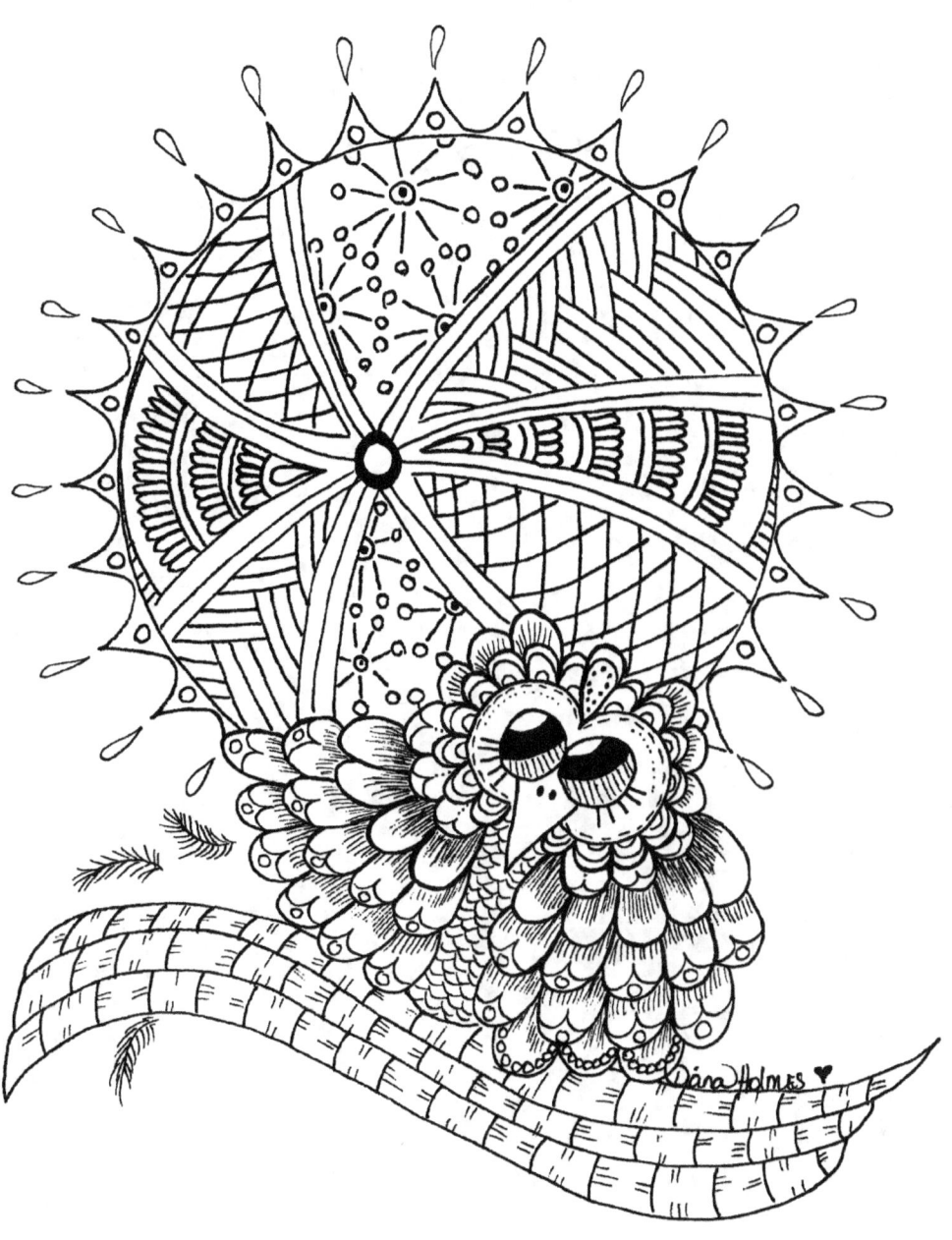

Contributing Artist
Joann Sands
Great Britain

Facebook :JSArt.Strokes

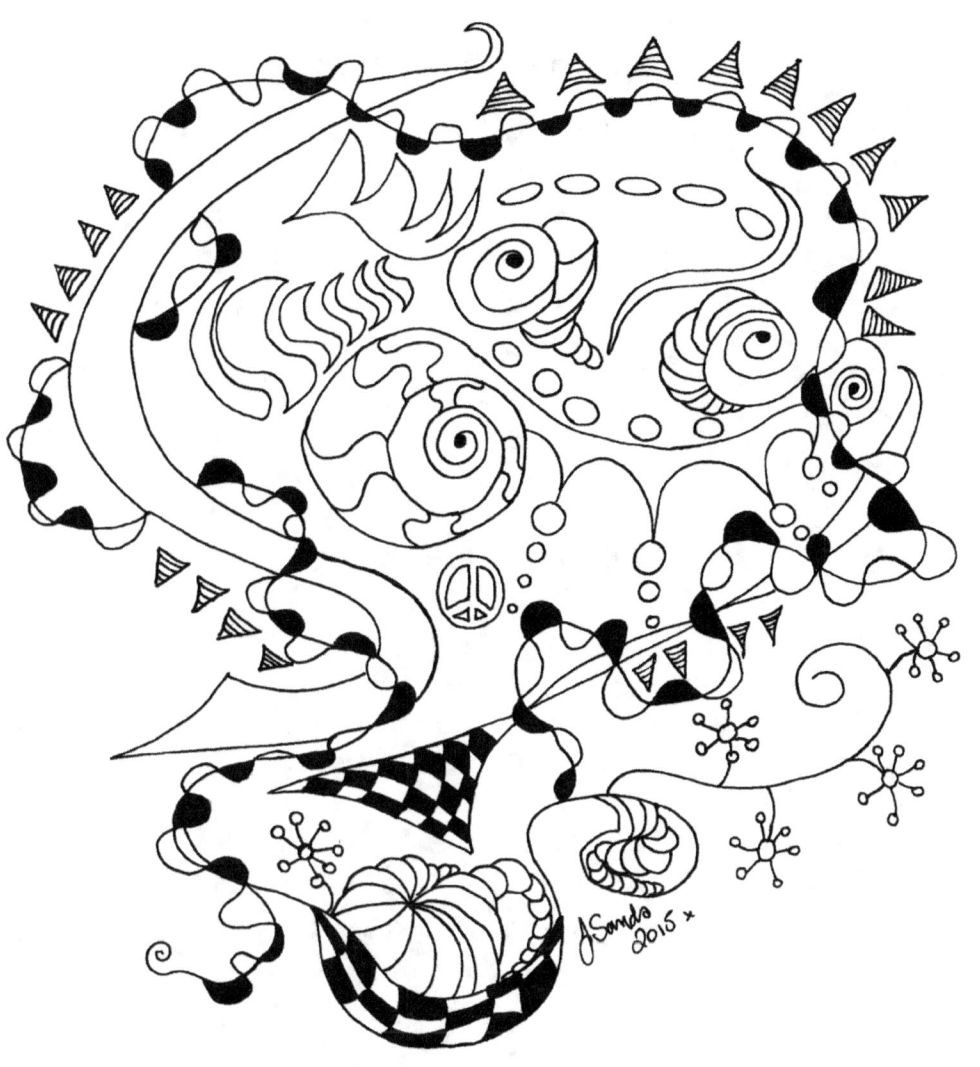

Contributing Artist
Jodi Ho
Taiwan

Facebook : riverho1688

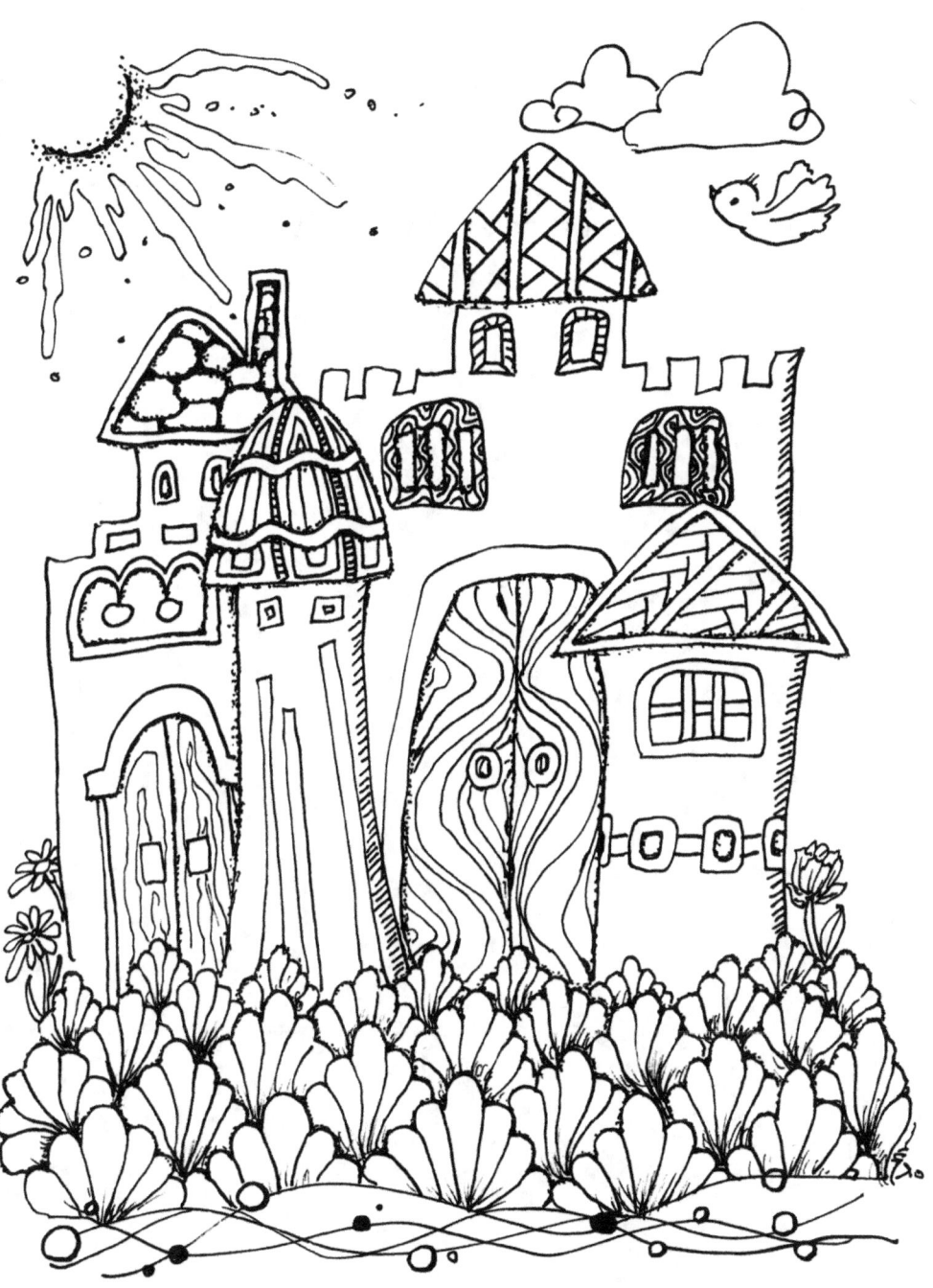

Contributing Artist
Lilan Chen
Taiwan

Facebook : lilanchen.art

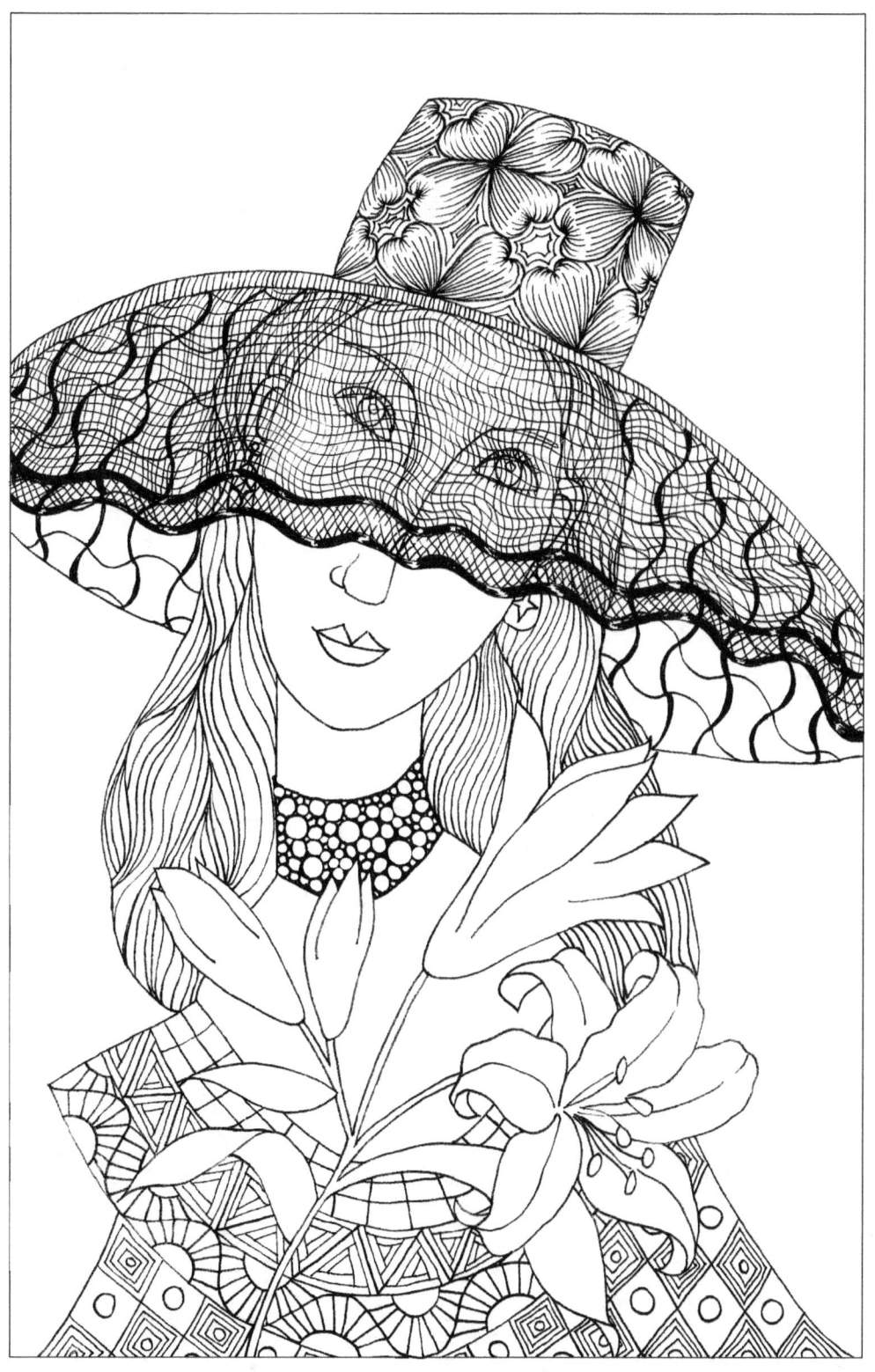

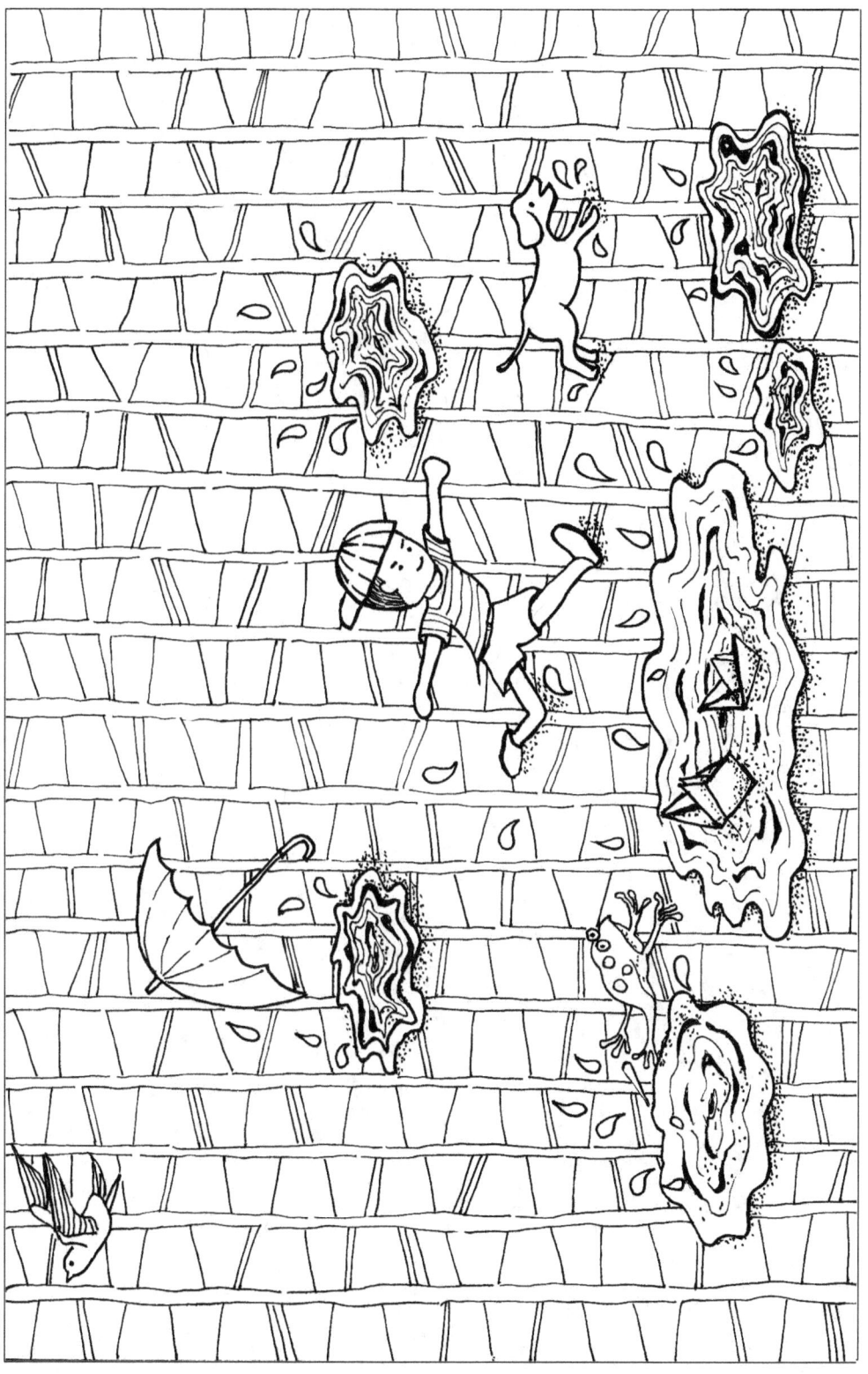

Contributing Artist
Lynne McGee
Brisbane, Australia

Facebook : Colorandtangle

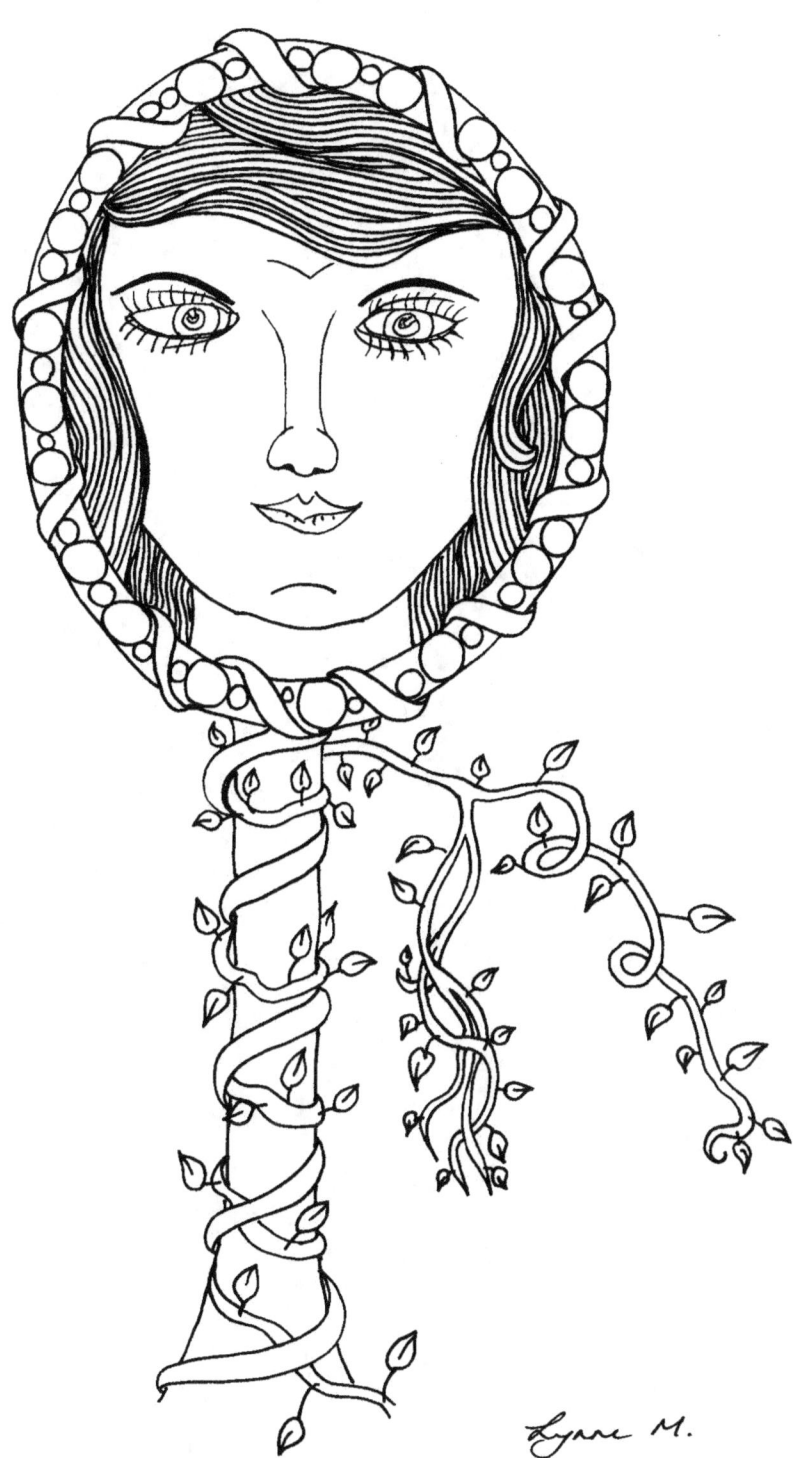

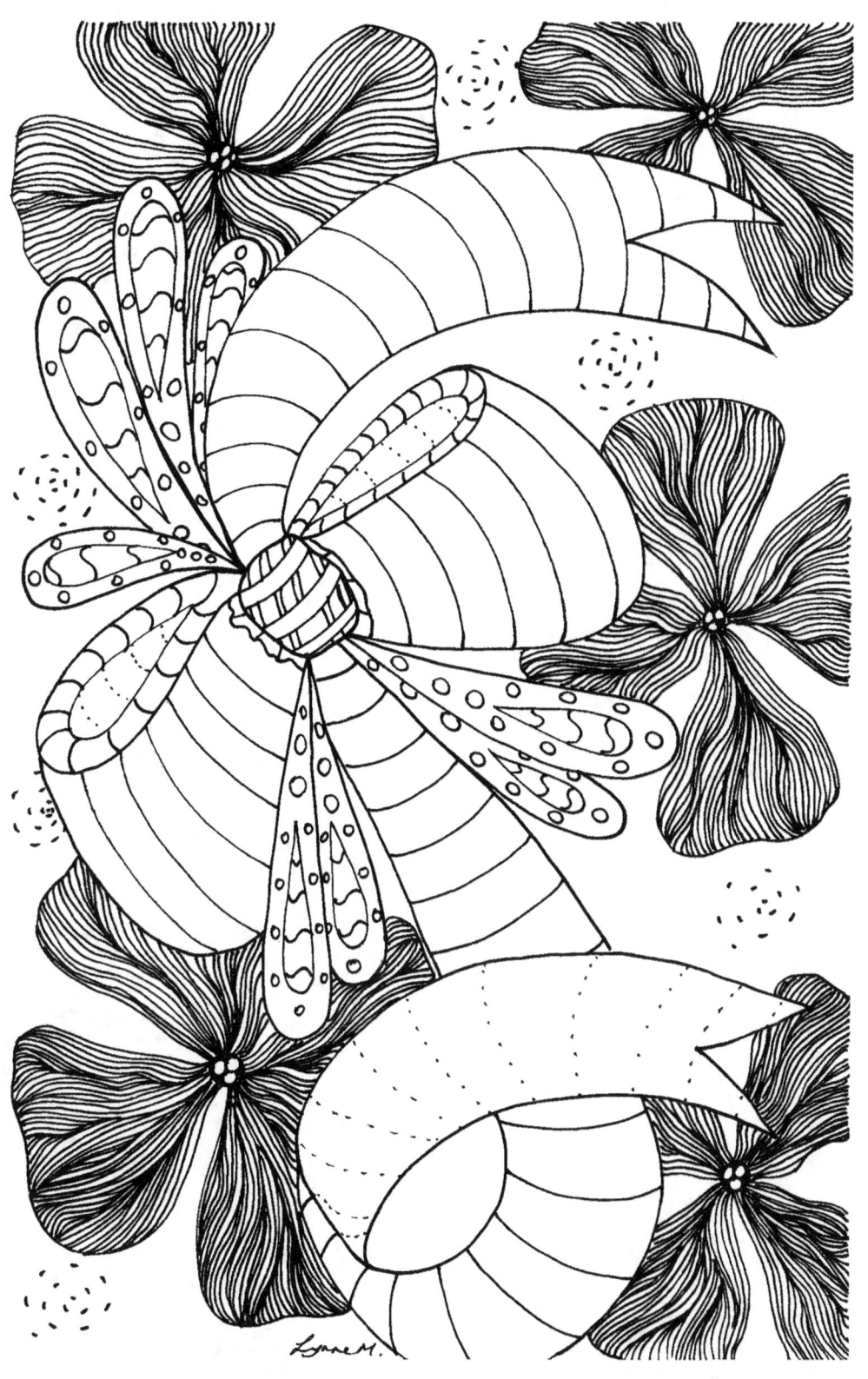

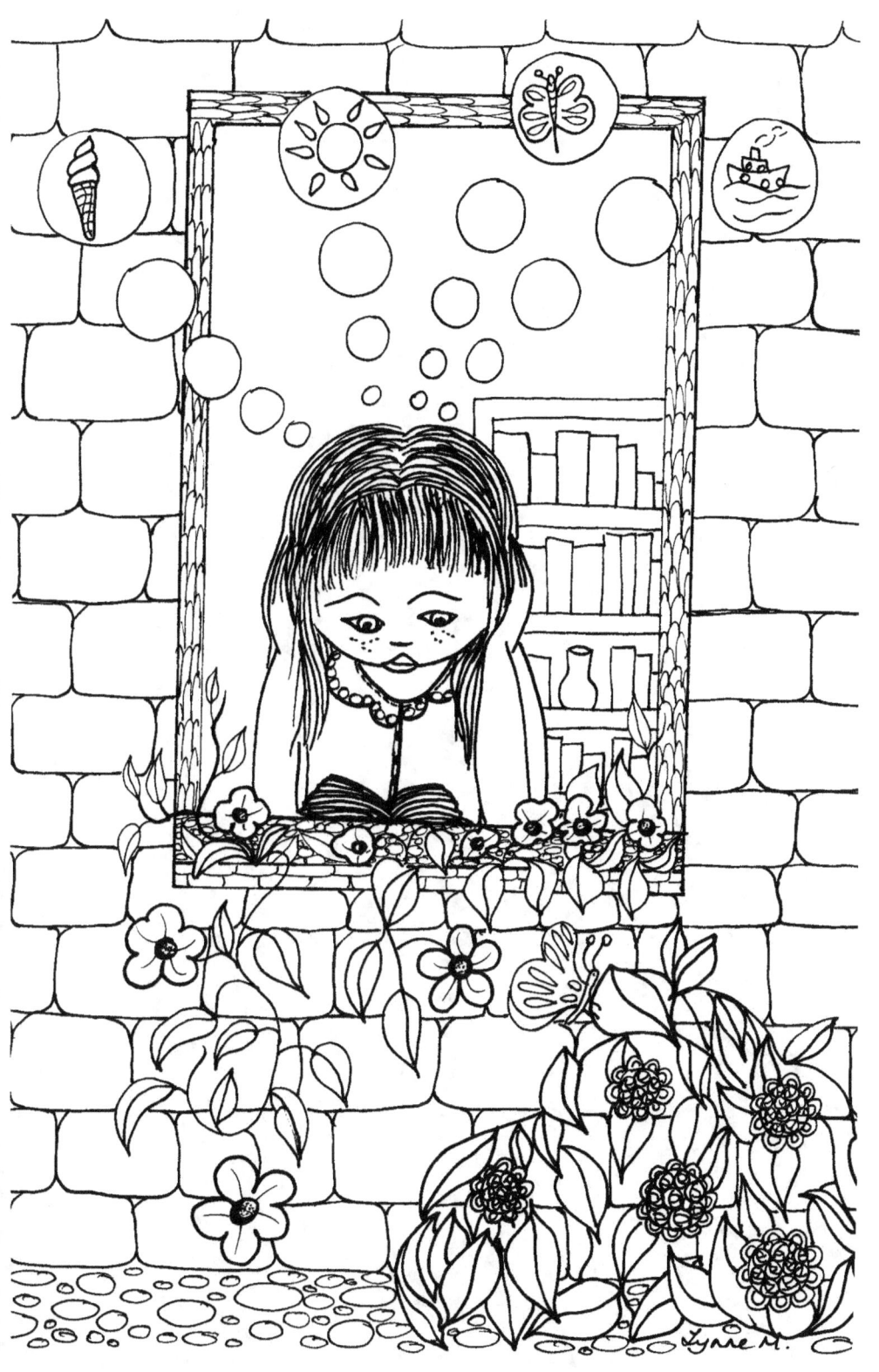

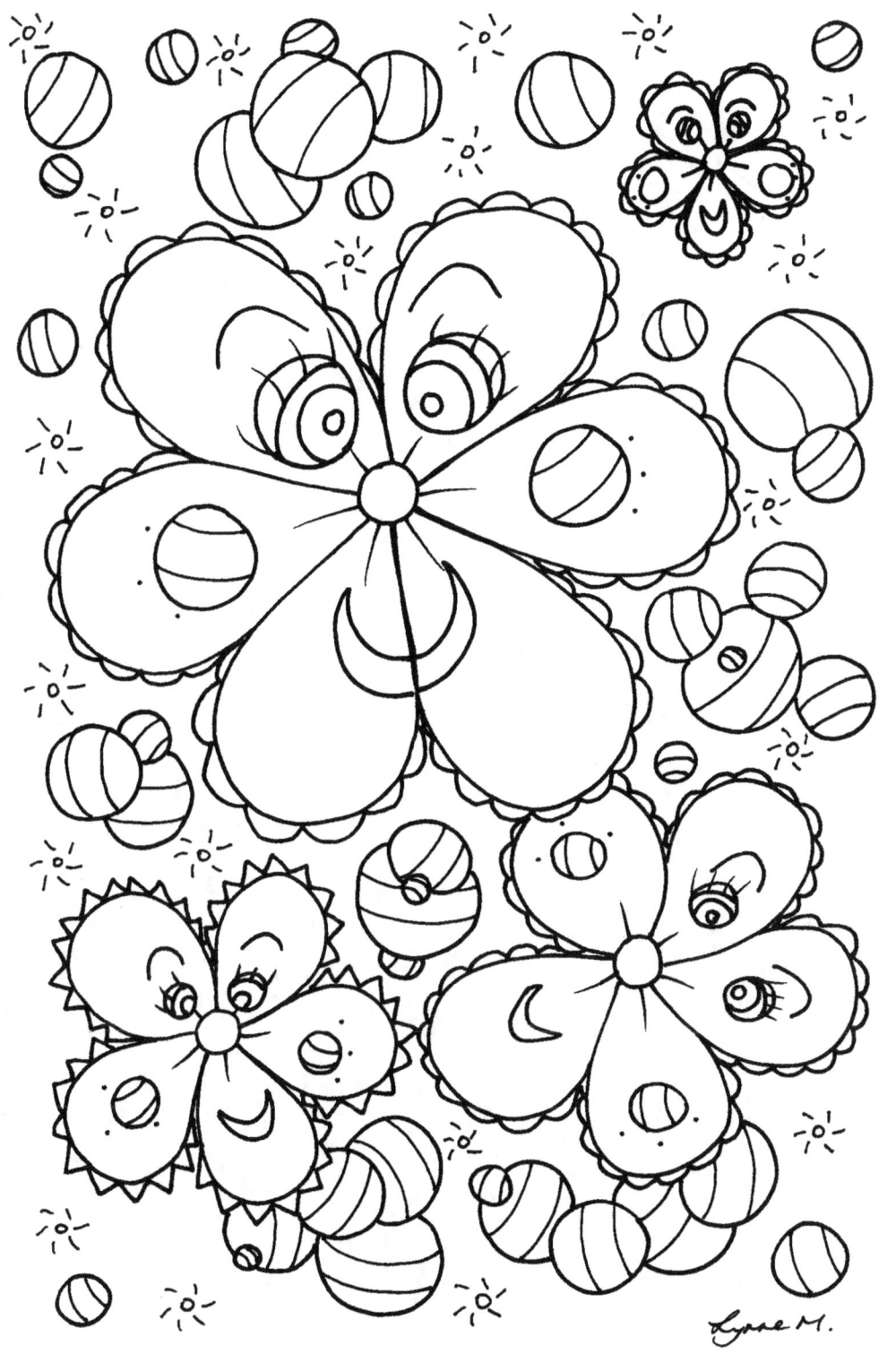

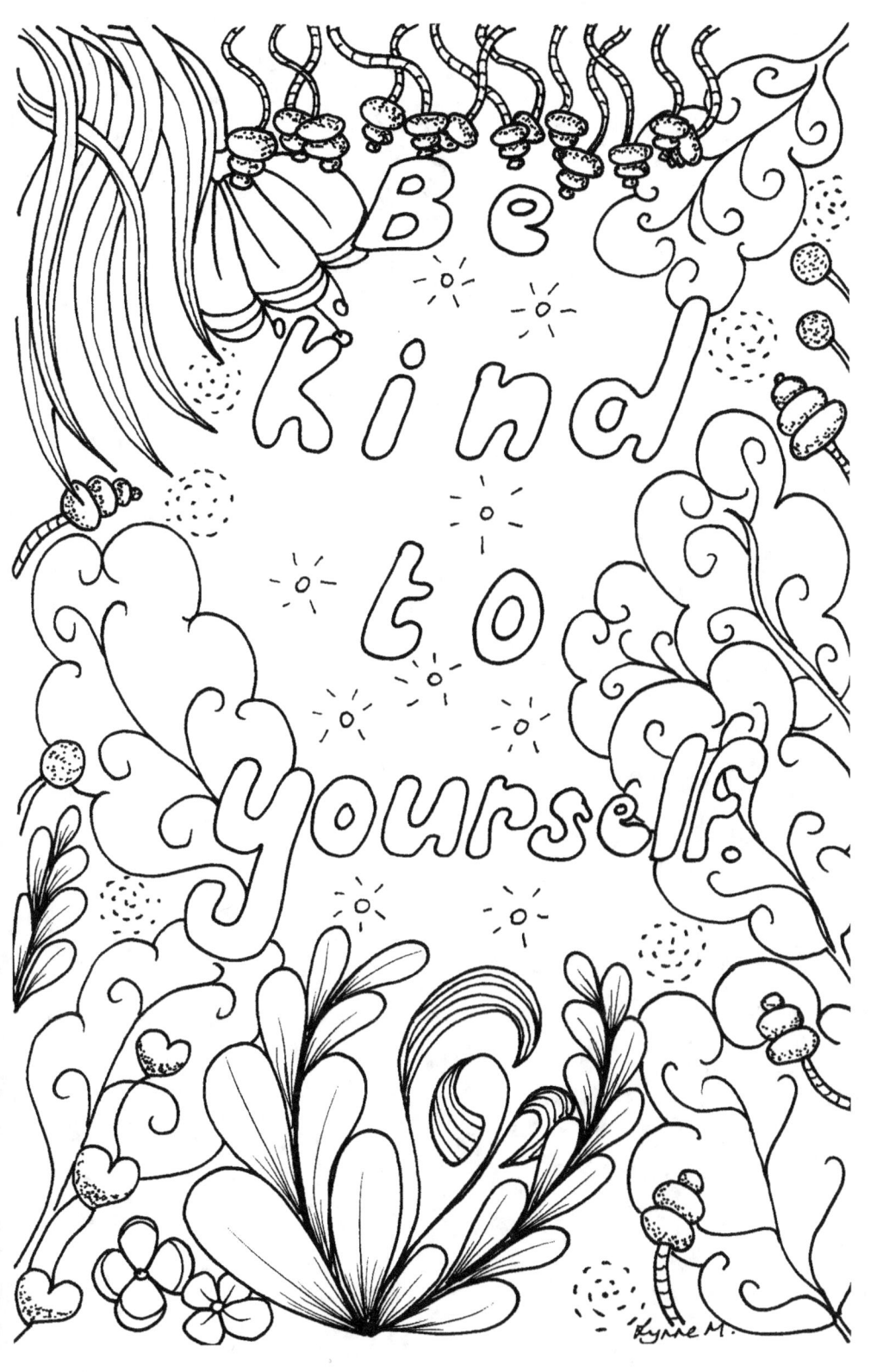

Contributing Artist
Nancy43
Taiwan

Facebook : 43Nancy43

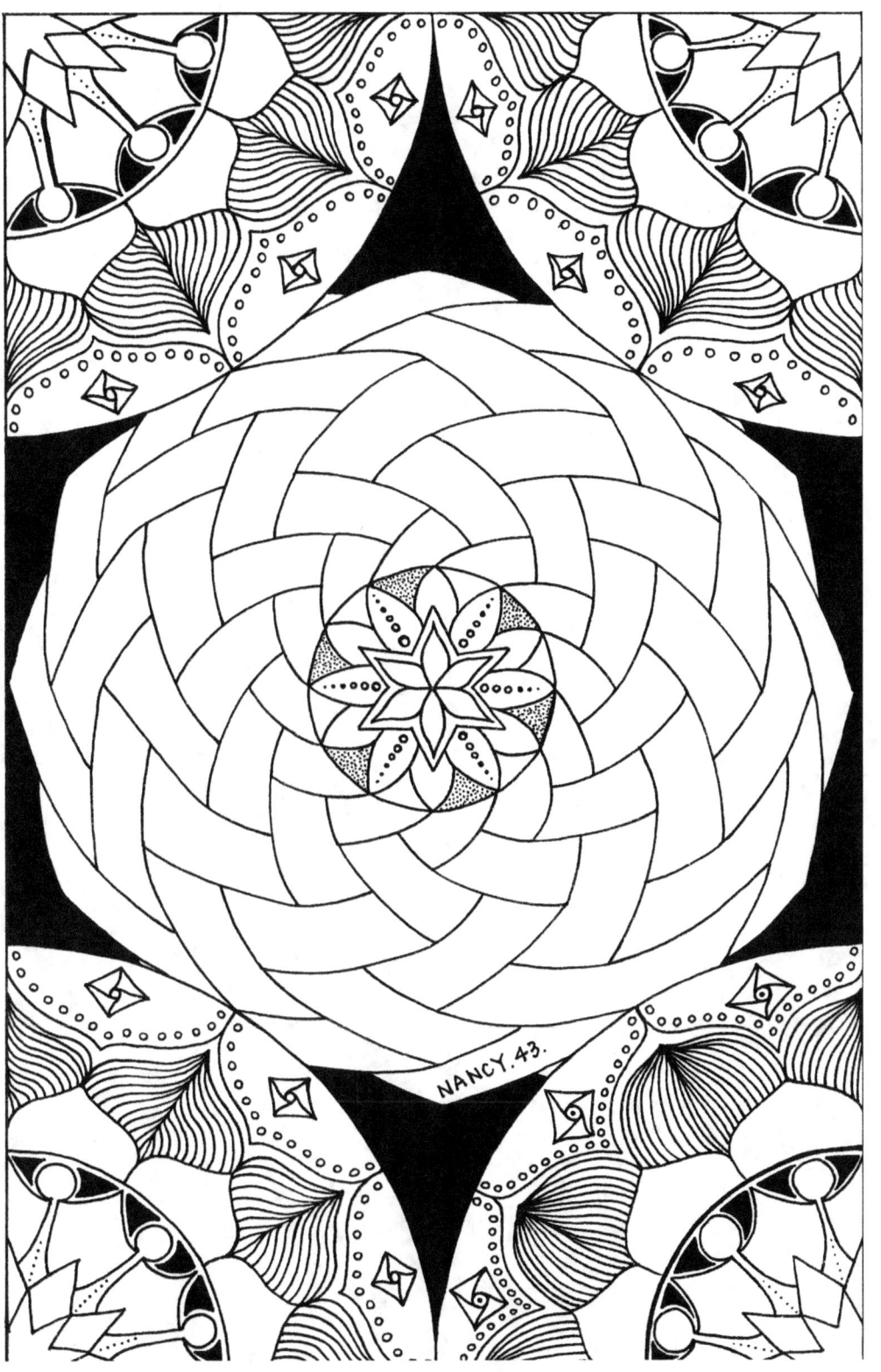

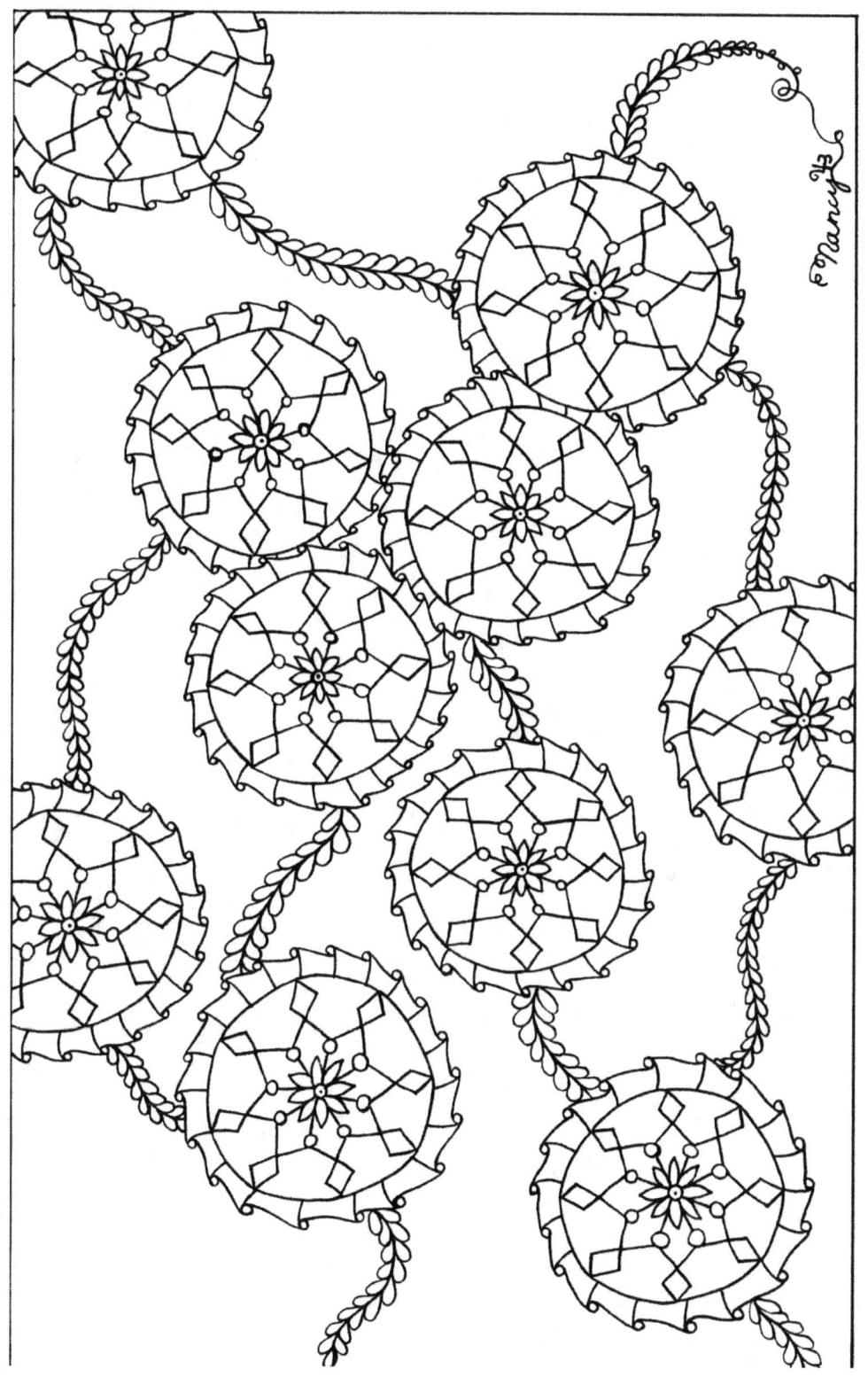

Contributing Artist
Pica Wu
Taiwan

Facebook : picapicadrow2

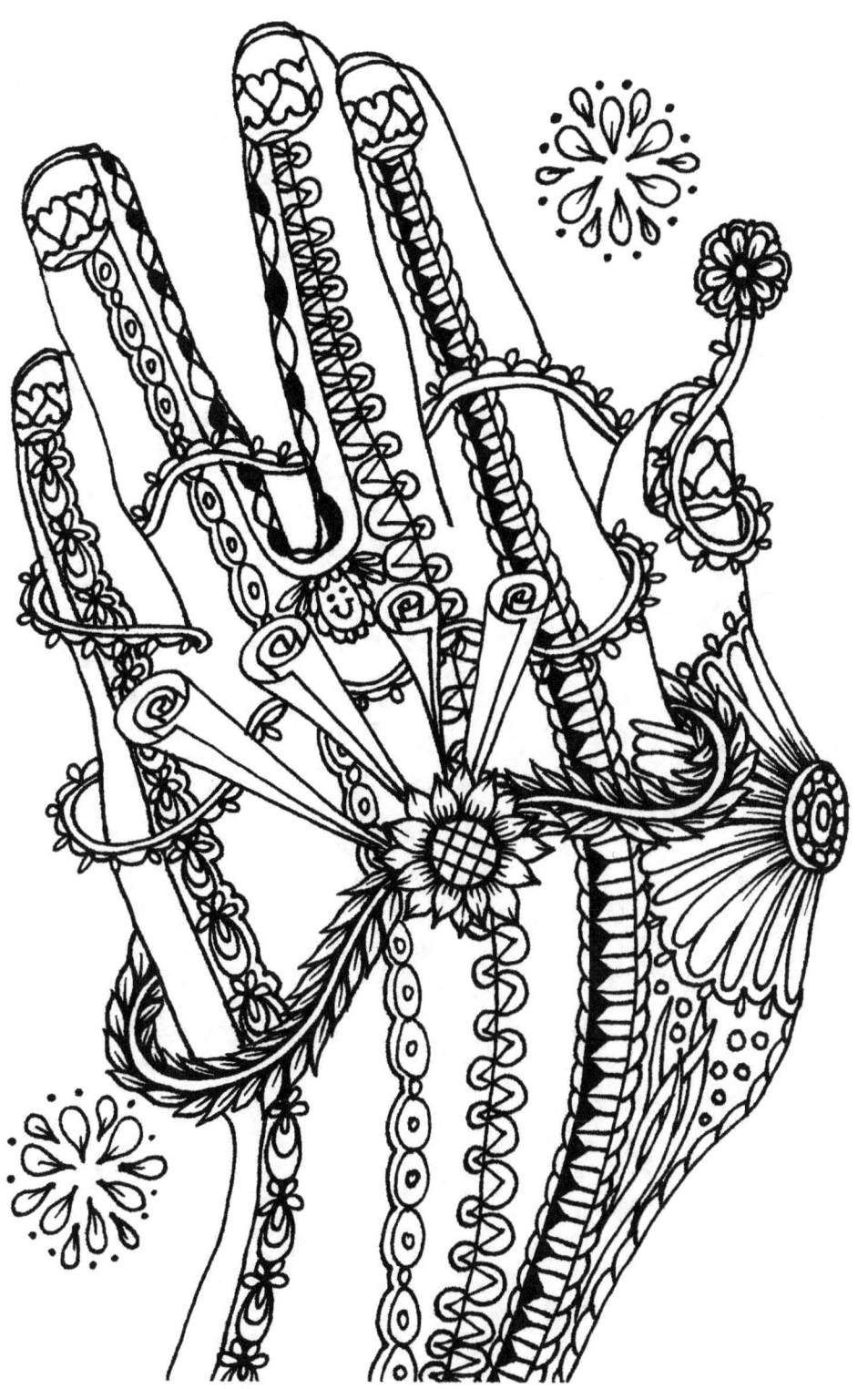

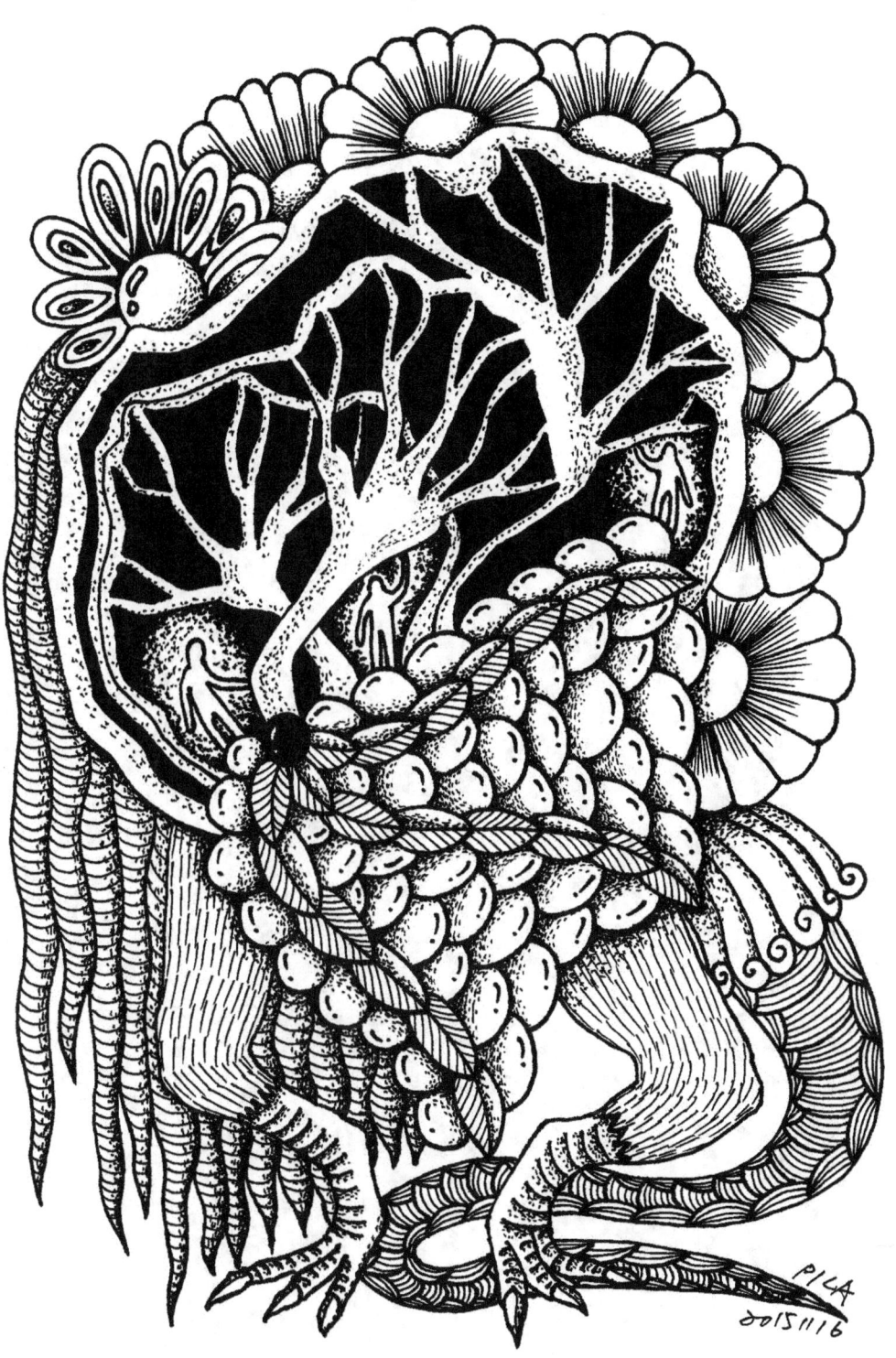

Contributing Artist
Rover Hsiao
Taiwan

Facebook : roverhsiao2015

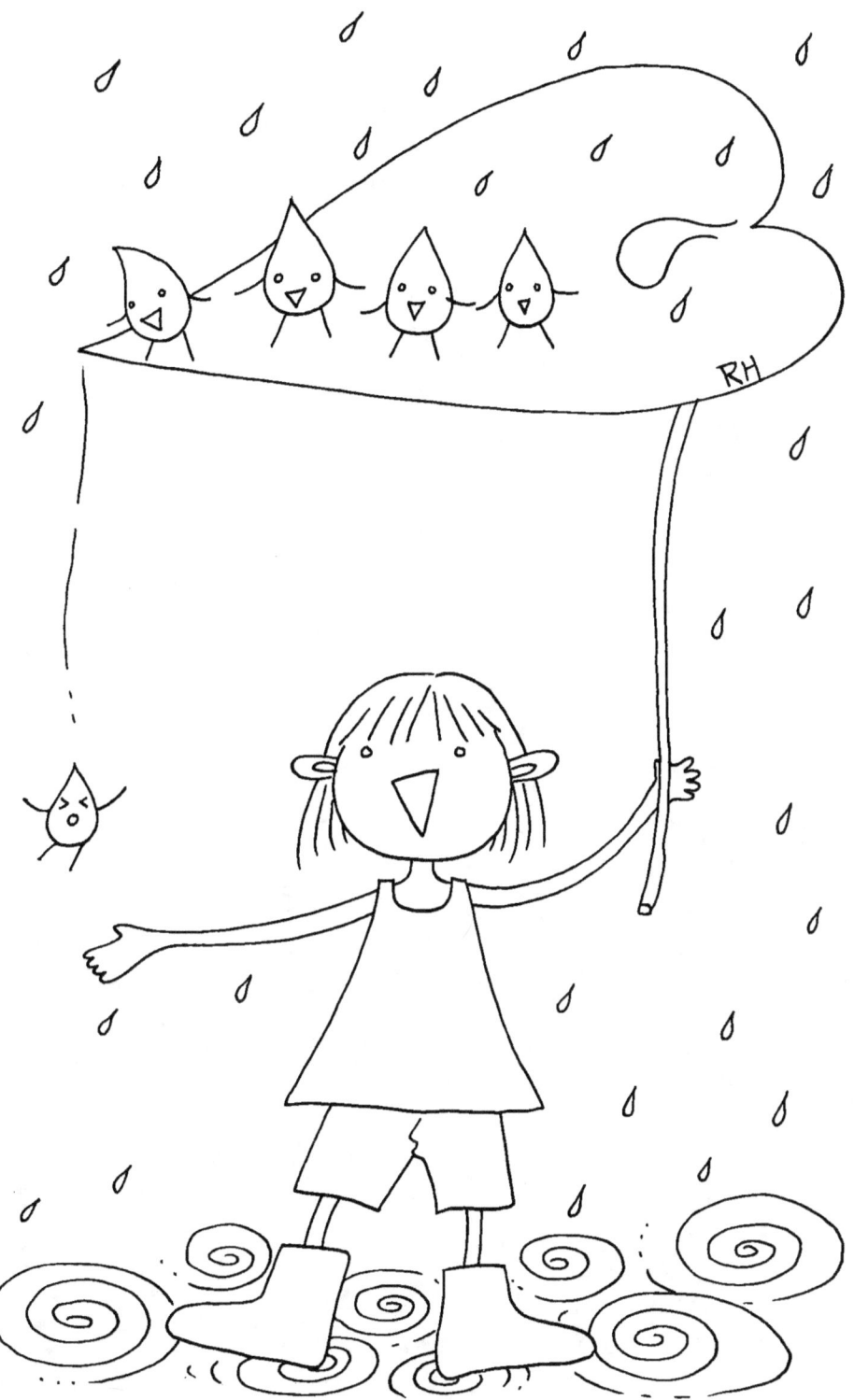

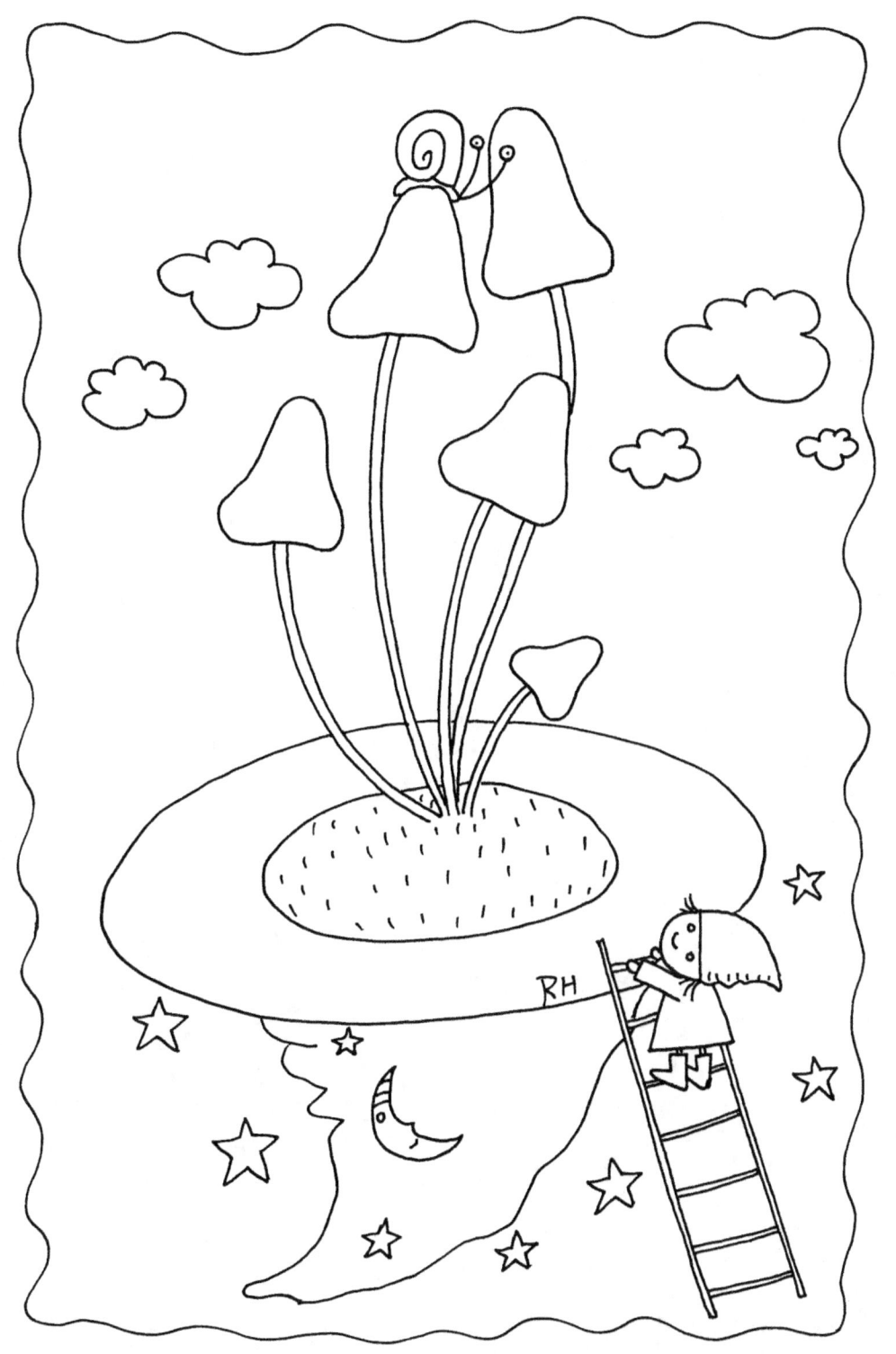

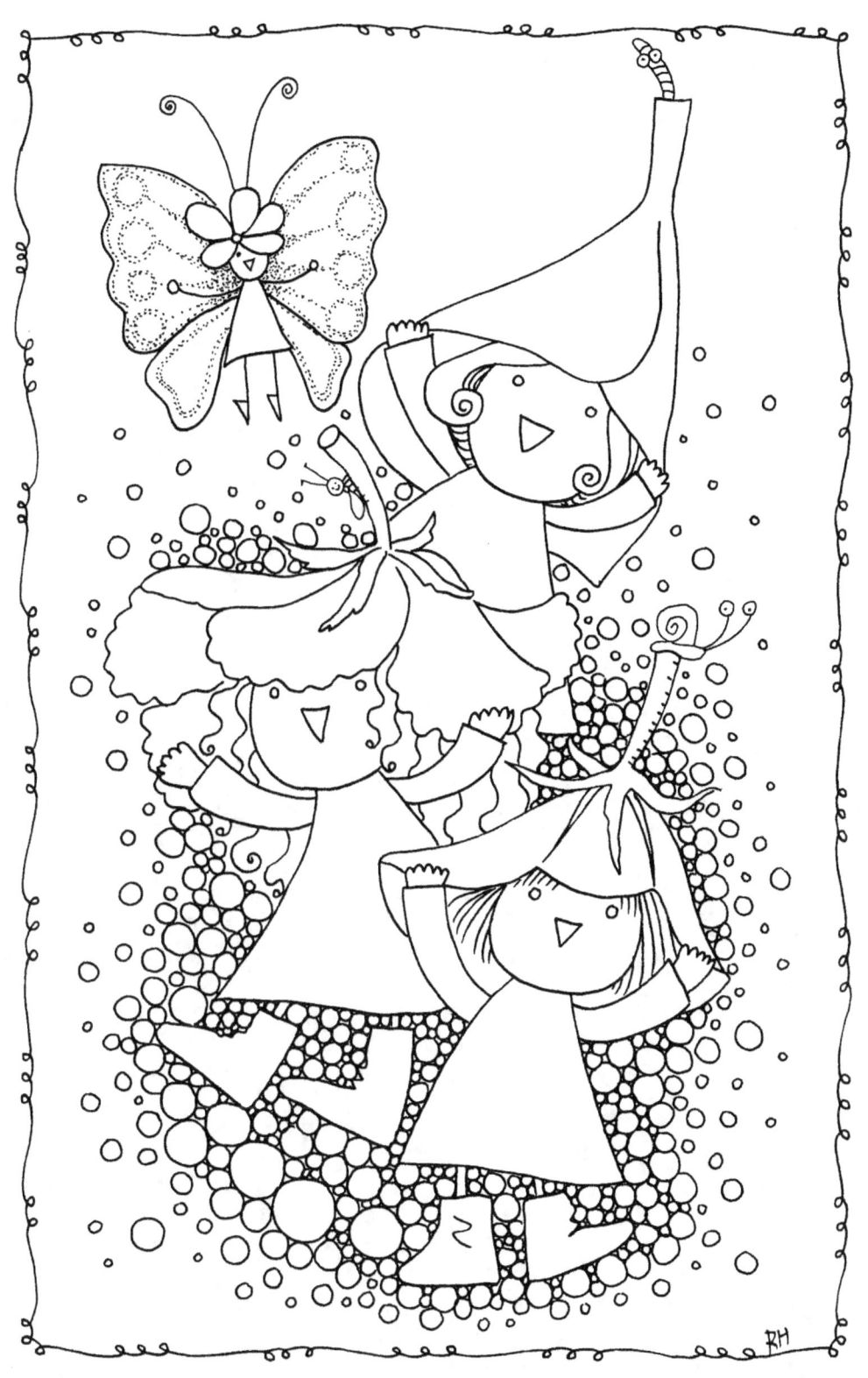

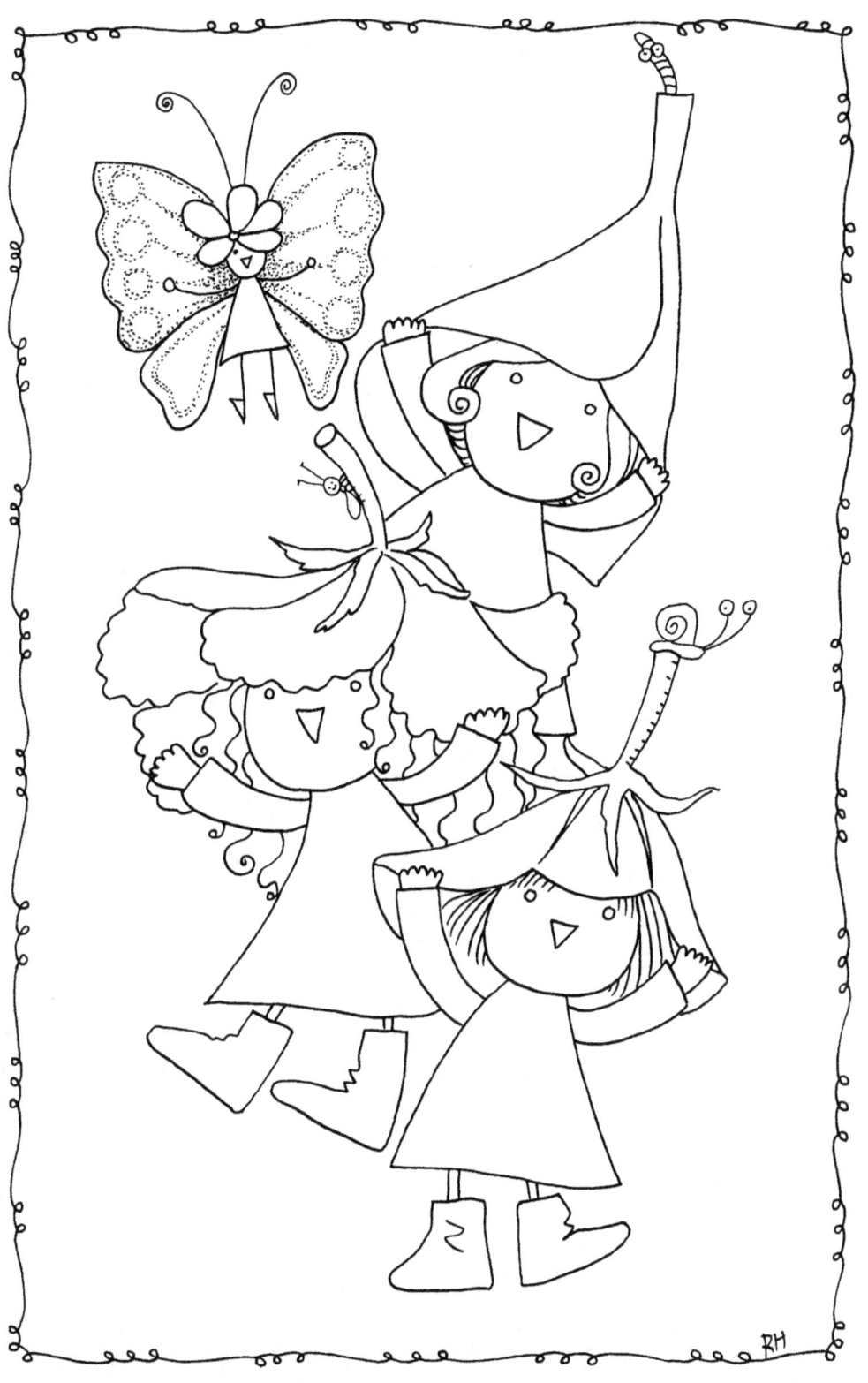

Contributing Artist
T.J.
USA

Facebook : TJsArtCorner

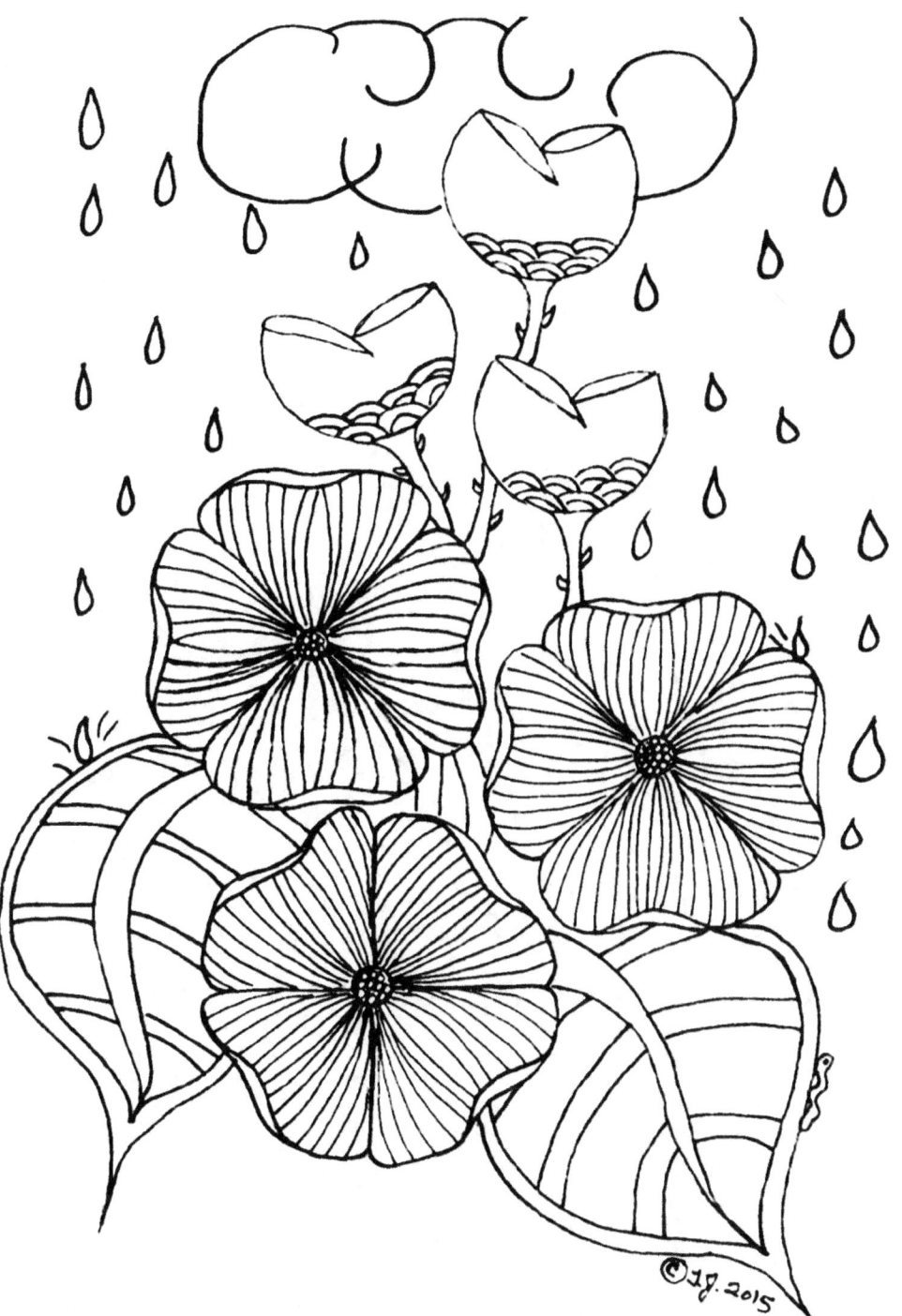

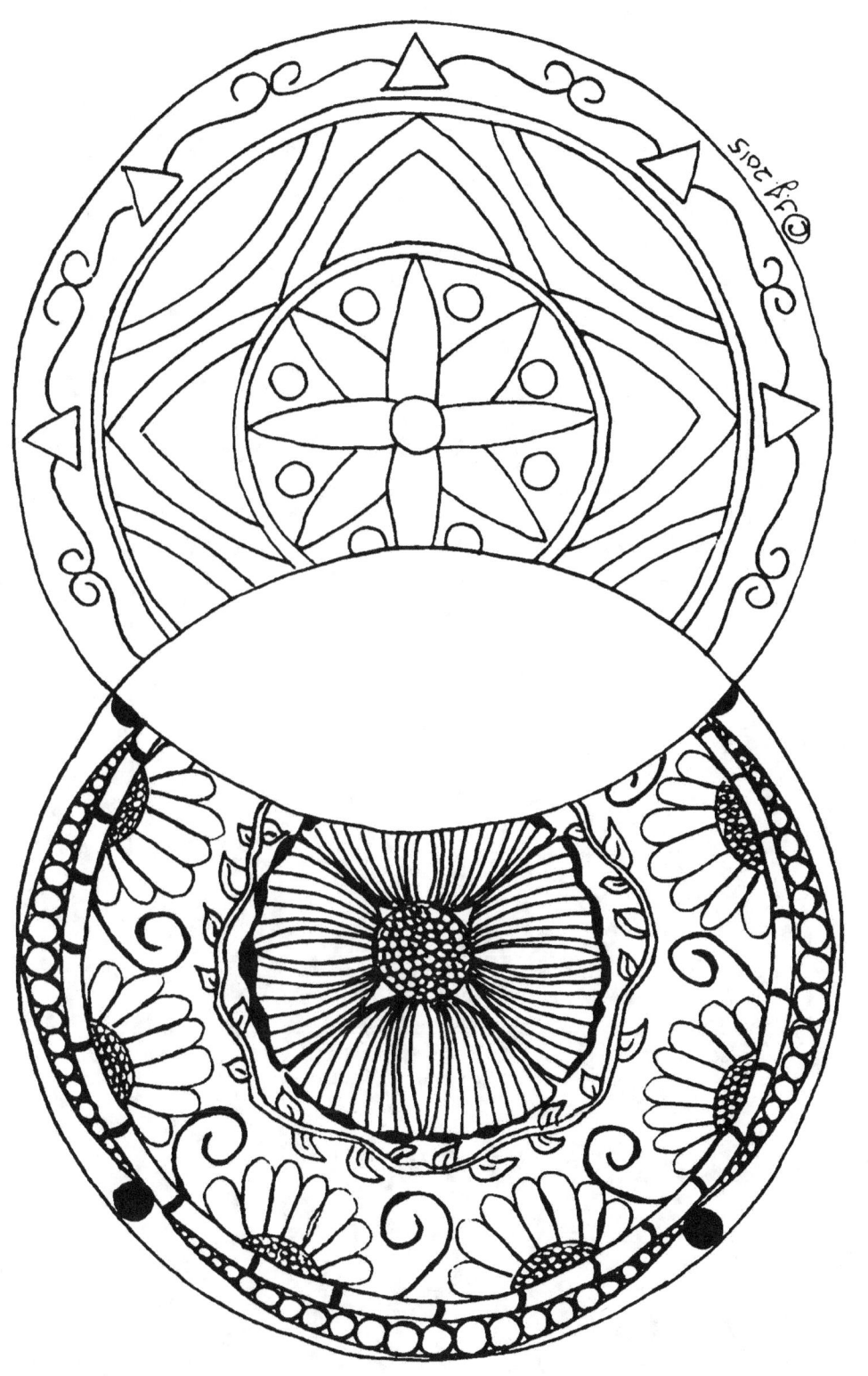

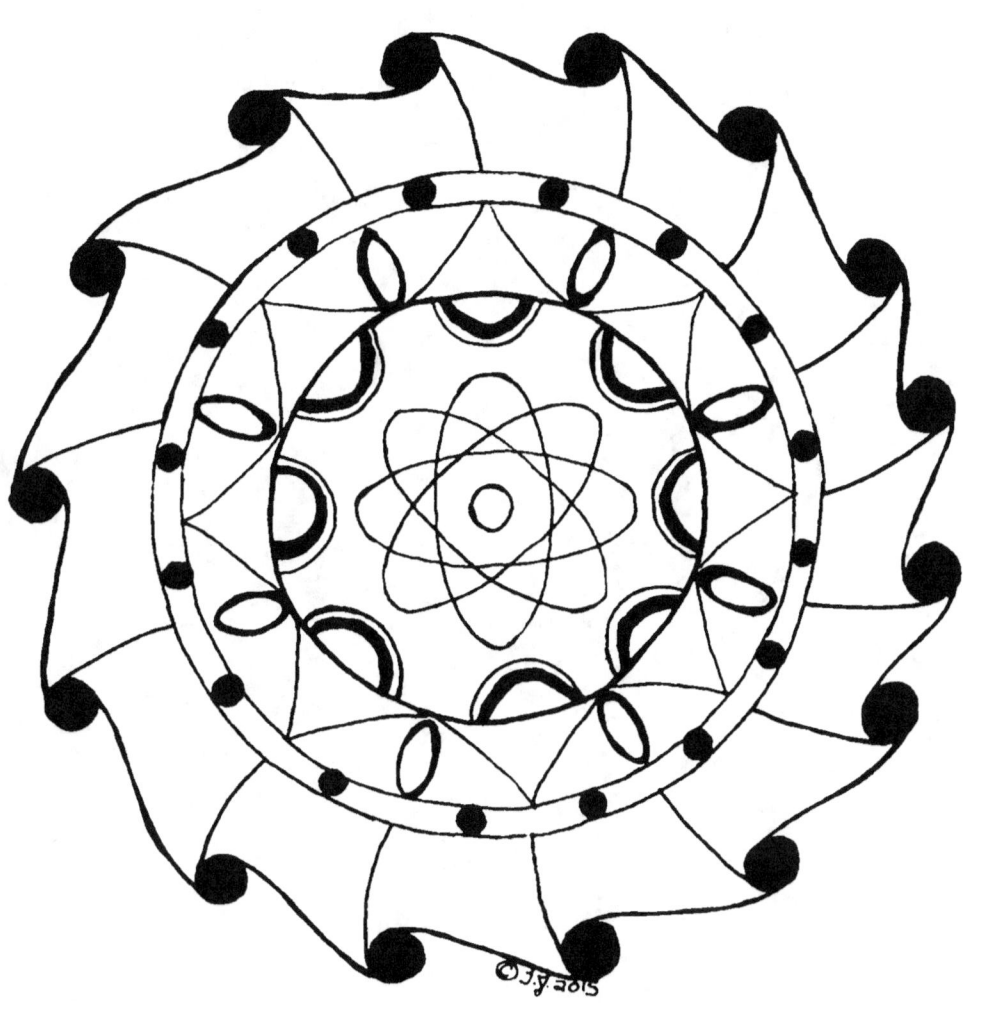

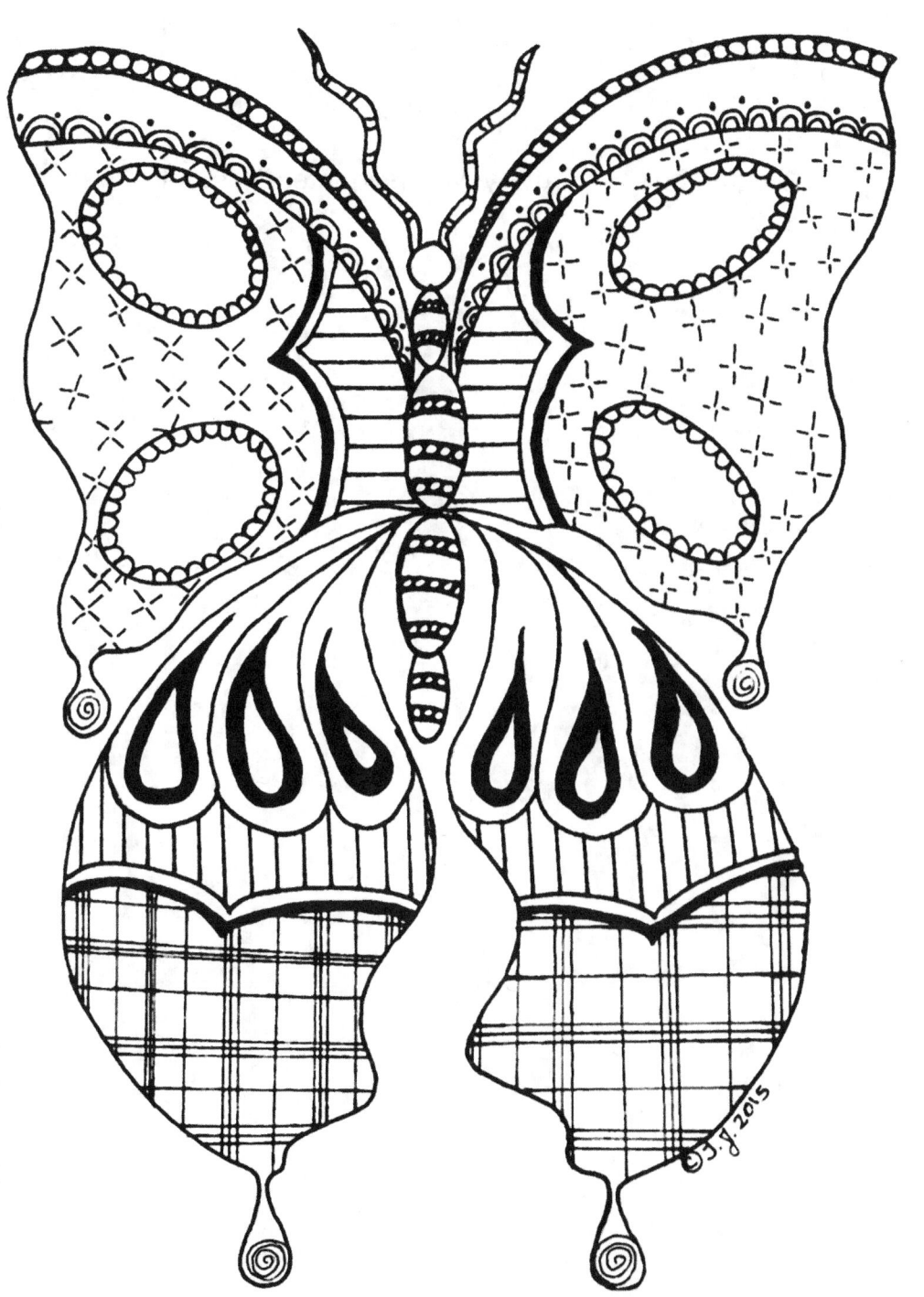

Contributing Artist
Mireille Westerduin, Colour by Mi
The Netherlands

Facebook : Colour-by-Mi-Kleurplaten-Illustraties

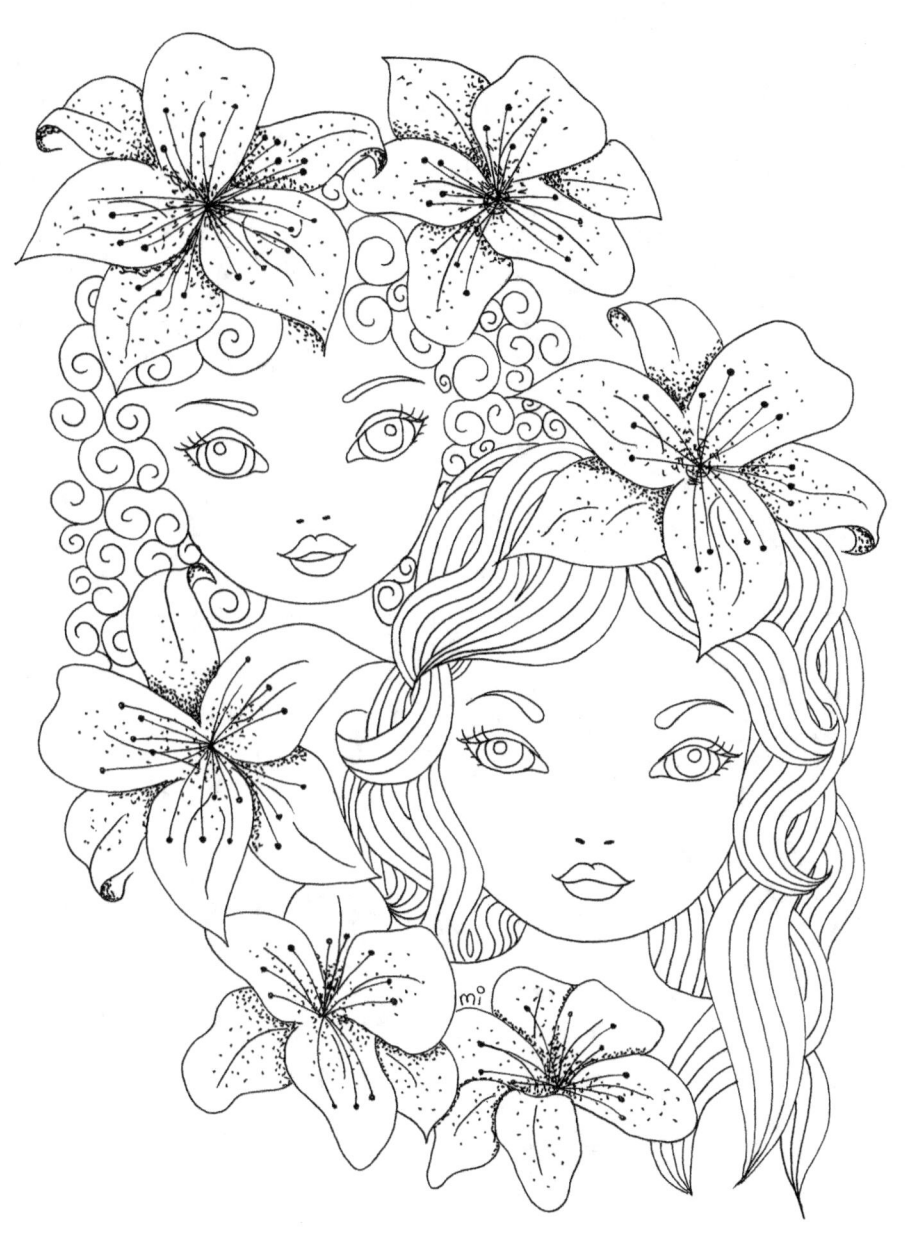

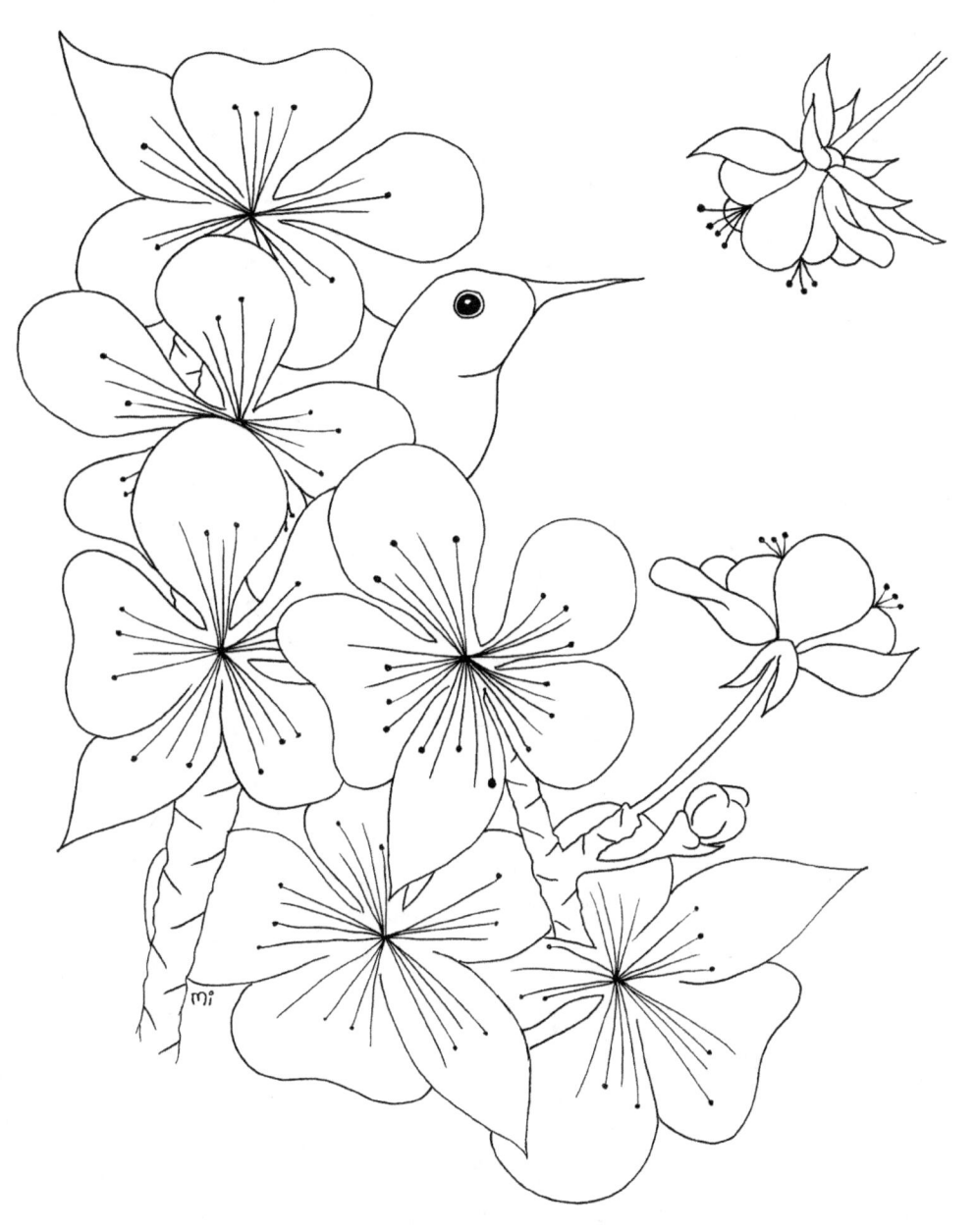

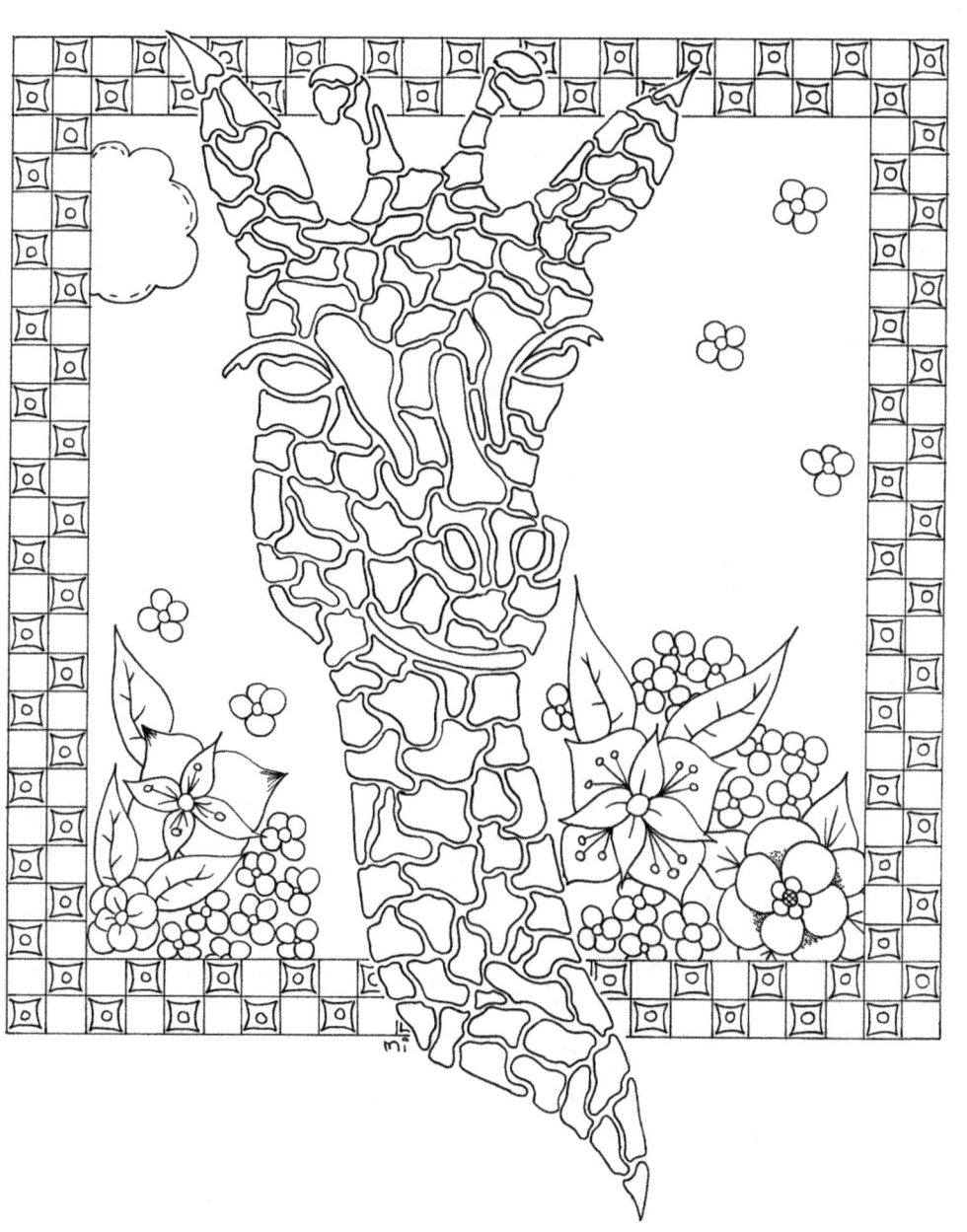

Contributing Artist
Nadège Zenfeerie
France

Facebook : zenfeerie

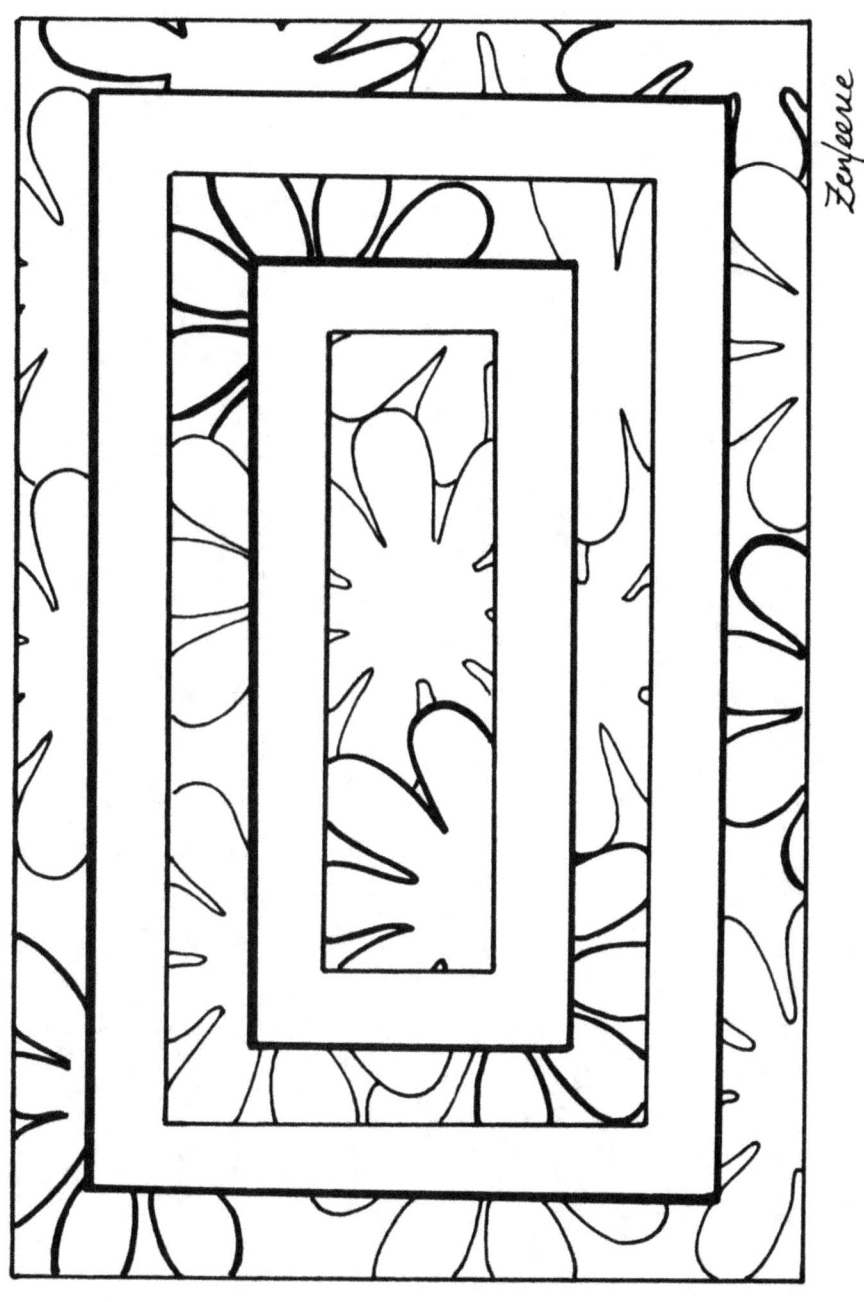

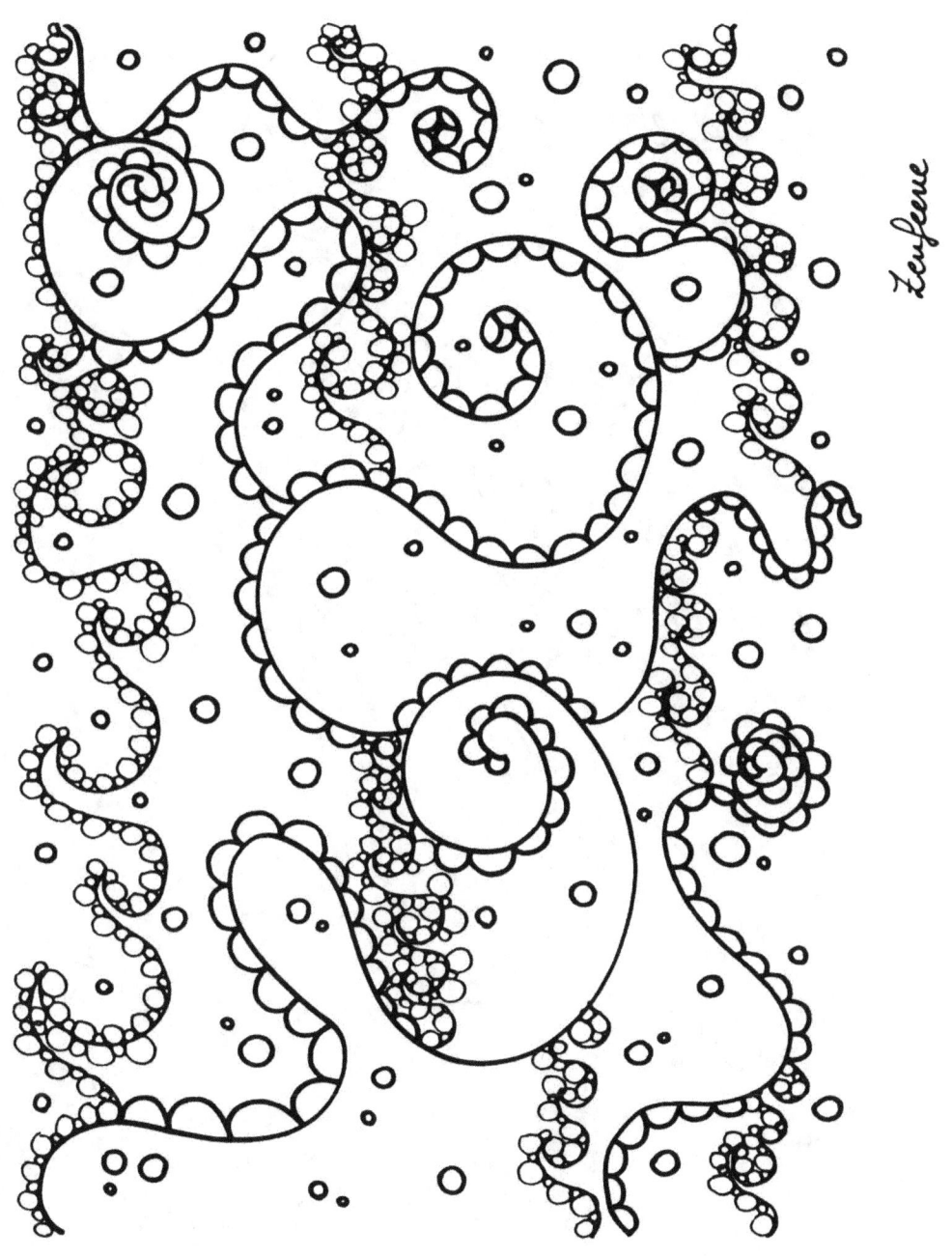

Drawn & Colored by Rover Hsiao

&

Drawn & Colored by Mireille W

Published by "GDG" Global Doodle Gems

www.ingramcontent.com/pod-product-compliance
Lightning Source LLC
Chambersburg PA
CBHW050116230526
45470CB00004B/1851